PRINTHOUSE BOOKS PRESENTS

Making Groceries
A Story of Creole Cooking from a Creole Family.
Cook Book

URSULA T. ROCHON

 Making Groceries
A Story of Creole Cooking from a Creole Family

Contents

Foreword ....page 8
Recipes from Mimi...page 9-15
Introduction to Creole Language……………………....……..page16-19

How to's and Short Cuts…
Make a stock (etc.)……………………………………….………page 22-23

Appetizers

Crawfish Bread…………………………………...…..………...page 26-27
Spinach Dip..page 28
Ursula's MAN dip...page 29
Lump Crabmeat and Artichoke Dip...page 31
Lump Crabmeat and Crawfish. ....page 32
Oyster Pies ....page 33
Crawfish Pies ....page 34
Hush Puppies ....page 35
Crab cakes..page 36
Crab Corn Soup..page 37
Corn Pudding...page 38

Contents

Sides

Jambalaya	page 41
Potato Salad	page 42
Sweet Potatoes	page 43
Auntie Mimi's Candied Yams in Orange Cups	page 44
Baked Green Beans	page 45
Stuffed Bell peppers	page 46
Stuffed Mirliton	page 47
Theresa's Baked Macaroni	page 48
Ursula's Shrimp Pasta	page 49
Grillades	page 50
Cowan	page 51
Mama Gourrier's Seafood Pasta	page 53-54
Assunta Gourrier's Yakamein	page 55
Ursula's famous Super Bowl wings	page 56

Contents

Main Courses

GUMBO
- Rochon Seafood Gumbo ...... page 59
- Turkey Sausage Gumbo ...... page 60
- Mimi's Okra Gumbo ...... page 61
- Gumbo Z'Herbs ...... page 62

BEANS
- White Beans ...... page 64
- Red Beans and Rice ...... page 65

SEAFOOD & MORE...
- Shrimp Étouffée' ...... page 66
- Crawfish Étouffée' ...... page 67
- Crawfish Bisque ...... page 68-70
- Crawfish Monica ...... page 71
- Crawfish Andouille Pasta ...... page 72
- Mom's Shrimp Creole ...... page 73
- Coubion ...... page 74
- Pane' Meat ...... page 75
- Oyster Rockefeller ...... page 76
- Baked Chicken and Gravy ...... page 77
- Smothered Chicken ...... page 78
- Alexis's Breaded Pork chops ...... page 79
- Ursula's Crockpot Roast ...... page 80
- Auntie Mimi's Baked Spaghetti & Meat Sauce ...... page 81
- Cabbage ...... page 82
- Fried Seafood Po-Boys ...... page 83
- Blackened Catfish ...... page 84
- Big Gio's Turkey Marinade ...... page 85
- Omari's Fried Turkey & Marinade ...... page 85
- Big Gio's Barbeque Chicken ...... page 86

Contents

Desserts

King Cake	page 89
White Chocolate King Cake	page 90
Super Easy Beignets	page 91
Pralines	page 92
Chocolate Chip Toffee Cookies	page 93
Rum Cake	page 94
Pecan Squares	page 95
White Chocolate Bread Pudding	page 96
King Cake Bread Pudding	page 97
Bananas Foster	page 98
Double Frosted Bourbon Brownies	page 99
Passé' Blanc Pecan Brownies	page 100
7up Pound Cake	page 101
Pumpkin's 7up Pound Cake	page 102
Dad's Pineapple Up-side Down Cake	page 103
Sweet Potato Pie	page 104
Babe's Favorite Pecan Pie	page 105
Peach Cobbler	page 106
Couzan Hazel's Lemon Meringue Pie	page 107-108
Thank You's	page 109-115
References	page 116
Notes for your own family recipes	page 117–136

©2015 URSULA T. ROCHON

Editor: Cheryl O. Hinton

Publication date: 8-15-2015

PrintHouse Books, Atlanta, GA.

www.PrintHouseBooks.com

VIP INK Publishing Group, Incorporated

All rights reserved. No parts of this book may be reproduced in any way, shape, form or by any means without permission in writing from the publisher or the author except by a reviewer.

Letter from the Author

A Louisiana Creole refers to people of any ancestry or mixture who are descended from settlers in the colonial French Louisiana region, before it became a part of the United States in 1803.

Creole cuisine is typical of these people. During the initial stage the colonization of Louisiana by the French Government, the French borrowed the term that the Spanish and Portuguese used in their colonies when referring to native-born products and people of the colony. The Spanish referred to this as *criollo*, and the Portuguese *crioule*. Ultimately, the colonial term derived from the Latin 'creare', meaning to rear or create. The Louisiana Creole people generally are combination of any of the following: French, Spanish, African, and/or Native American. Most reside in or have familial ties to Louisiana.

With that said…….
This cookbook, is dedicated to everyone that left New Orleans at one point or another, and was asked the question…"What are you mixed with?"

After the hurricane it seems as if we all miss *home*. We all want to go *home*, we all can't wait until it's the way it used to be and we can return *home*. Well *home* is not New Orleans, it's the food we had in New Orleans. It's the fun we had cooking and eating before, during, and after every party. *Home* is the crawfish boils at Mardi Gras, and the shrimp Creole on Sunday after Church, and the Red beans on Monday. *Home* is the first time you watched your grandma make pralines. *Home* is rum cakes and bread pudding and the good ole dinner rolls from you know where. We all miss *home* but there is no reason why we can't celebrate *home* right where we are no matter where it is. As long as you have good food and family trust me you are *home*!
For everyone, that misses *home*, this is for you…

Laissez les bons temps rouler !!!

Foreword

Vibration cooking is a term my grandmother would give when you would ask her how to cook something.

" Mimi this is so good how did you make it, what did you put in it?"
" Oh sweetie I don't know a little of this a little of that, it's called vibration cooking."

It's not about what you put in it, it's all in , *"how you hold your mouth when you stir the pot."*
~Mimi

So essentially, with Creole cooking there really is no recipe. <u>Creole cooking comes from the heart, there is no recipe or guideline to follow, you just do it</u>. You add a pinch of this or pinch of that until you get it right. You will notice that all of the following recipes, either have no measurement, or they refer to the ingredients as a bunch of this or a pinch of that.

That's how the recipes are passed down from generation to generation, they are taught in the kitchen, they aren't passed down on paper. Since Creole cooking comes from the heart it would be too impersonal to pass it down on paper. Each generation has a story of how they "used to" help in the kitchen while their parents or grandparents were cooking. Everything from greasing the Bundt pan for the rum cake, to chopping the seasoning to add to the Shrimp Creole. All those steps, were how we learned to cook. To make your life easier The rest of the cookbook isn't written like this. You may come across a recipe where I didn't give a measurement, "eyeball it," and use your best judgment. This cookbook is not for the lighthearted but your are welcome to have fun with it anyway. This foreword is a dedication to all those generations of cooking and the people who learned to cook like that. I would like to dedicate this portion of the book to "Mimi" Ursula Carrere Jupiter, "T~Mimi" Muriel Revels, and my parents, Gregory and Janet Rochon , for teaching me how to cook by adding a pinch of something and a bunch of everything else.

Thank you!

"Recipes from Mimi"

Jambalaya

"It's all in how your hold your mouth when you stir the pot."

Onion
Green onion
Bell pepper
Parsley
Tomato Paste
Tomato Sauce
Turkey Sausage
Beef Sausage
Shrimp
Rice (white or brown)

Sauté onions, garlic, bell pepper, parsley, and tomato paste. After completely sautéed add tomato sauce. After about 10 minutes add a small amount of water and let simmer for about 10 additional minutes. This is a good time to brown your sausage.

Once your meat is brown, add meat and shrimp to tomato sauce. Add salt and pepper to taste. Cayenne if desired.

Lower heat and add rice stir often until rice is fully cooked.

Pasta Jambalaya

Substitute with Pasta in place of rice for Pasta Jambalaya.

Make sure that pasta is cooked al dente' that way it will not turn mushy once mixed with the sauce.

Rochon Seafood Gumbo

Onions, diced
Green bell peppers, diced
Garlic, minced
Shrimp stock, crab stock or fish stock
Creole seasoning blend
Bay leaves
Turkey sausage
Filé, Cayenne pepper, salt and black pepper to taste
Shrimp, peeled and de-veined
Oysters, freshly shucked, liquor reserved
Blue crabs, cleaned (optional)
Fresh lump crabmeat, picked over for shells and cartilage
Filé powder
Cooked long-grain white rice

Chop all of your seasonings and set aside for later. Cut the turkey sausage into pieces. Brown and set aside for later

Make your roux, and then once roux is brown add vegetables. Sauté' the vegetables in the roux, and then add to stock. Bring all ingredients to a boil sand then reduce the heat and continue to cook for an additional 30 minutes. Add whole blue crabs. Remove the hard top shell from the crabs (do not throw AWAY, I am sure you know they make for good stock) and break each crab in two down the middle. Remove the claws. Add to the stock.) With the gumbo on very low heat, add the shrimp 10 minutes before serving, the oysters and oyster liquor 5 minutes before serving, and the crabmeat just before serving (don't cook the crabmeat, just stir until it is heated through). Don't forget your file'.

Red Beans and Rice

Red Kidney Beans
Onions
Parsley
Garlic
Green Onion
Salt
Black Pepper
Cayenne Pepper
Sausage
(if you want the healthier version try turkey sausage it tastes just as good)

In a large stock pot bring water to a boil. Cut Onions in quarters and drop tem in. Yes, I said it, drop them in. They don't have to be cut fine, so why waste your time doing so.

In a separate frying pan sauté green onion, garlic, and parsley; add this to the boiling water and onions.

At this point you should add your red beans to the boiling water.

In the same pan brown your sausage. To give the sausage a good flavor, leave some of the sautéed seasoning in the frying pan, once the sausage is brown, add it to the beans.

Sausage tip: *Make sure the sausage is brown on both sides; otherwise it will get soggy once it's sits in the beans.*

Towards the end once the beans are almost done, remove a spoonful of the red beans and smash them in a cup. Add gravy as you smash the beans. Once the beans are fully smashed and mixed with the gravy you have removed from the stock pot return it back to the pot. This will make them creamy. YUM!

Oyster Pie

Oysters - heat, cook until curl up —

Roux of flour & butter
cook onions in roux
add celery & green onions
cook. for 5 min
add oysters not water
parsley, thyme, bay leaf
& worchester sauce
cook on low heat
add liquid
Cook in unbaked pie
shell 400° 35 to 40 min

1 double pie shell
4 doz. lg. oysters
1 stick flour
1 stick butter
1/2 onion
1/2 cup celery
1/2 cup green onions
2 tablespoon parsley
1 teaspoon thyme
1 teas worchester sauce

Making Groceries
A Story of Creole Cooking from a Creole Family

NEW ORLEANS PRALINES

2 STICKS BUTTER
2 CUPS CREAM
2 CUPS LIGHT BROWN
2 TABLESPOON (WHITE) SUGAR
     (CORN SYRUP)
4 CUPS SUGAR
8 CUPS PECANS

MIX AND COOK, BUTTER, CREAM, BROWN SUGAR, CORN SYRUP (W) SUGAR 15 OR 20 MIN. - STIRRING CONTINIOUSLY - UNTIL SUGAR FORMS A FIRM BALL WHEN DROPPED INTO COLD WATER. THEN ADD PECANS TO MIXTURE - STIRRING RAPIDLY A FEW MIN. - REMOVE FROM HEAT AND PUT OUT WITH TABLESPOON ON WAX PAPER - PLACED OVER THREE LAYERS OF NEWSPAPER. REMOVE WHEN FIRM OR HARD.

Making Groceries
A Story of Creole Cooking from a Creole Family

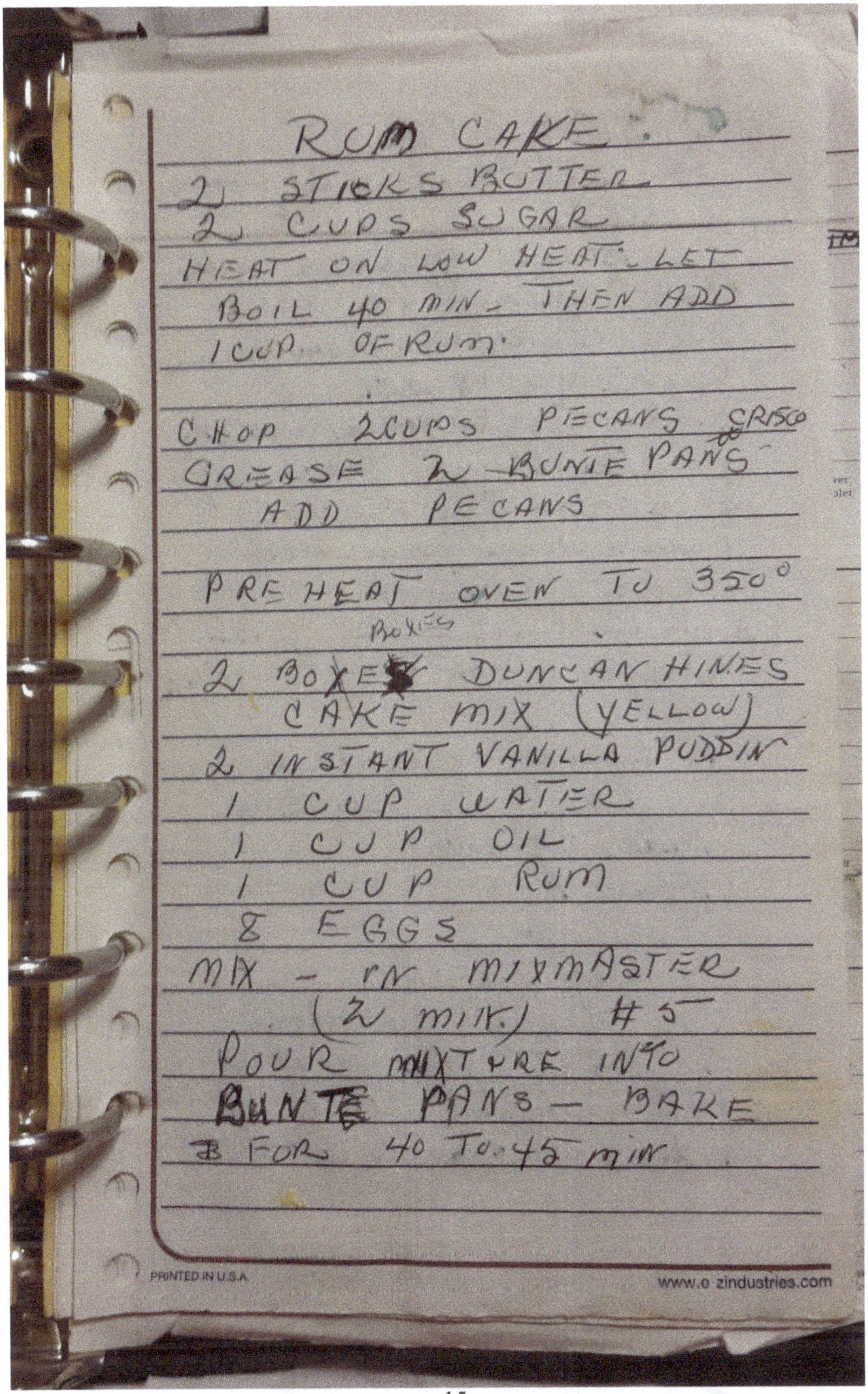

RUM CAKE

2 STICKS BUTTER
2 CUPS SUGAR
HEAT ON LOW HEAT. LET
BOIL 40 MIN. THEN ADD
1 CUP OF RUM.

CHOP 2 CUPS PECANS CRISCO
GREASE 2 BUNTE PANS
ADD PECANS

PRE HEAT OVEN TO 350°

2 BOXES DUNCAN HINES
CAKE MIX (YELLOW)
2 INSTANT VANILLA PUDDIN
1 CUP WATER
1 CUP OIL
1 CUP RUM
8 EGGS
MIX - IN MIXMASTER
(2 MIN.) #5
POUR MIXTURE INTO
BUNTE PANS - BAKE
B FOR 40 TO 45 MIN

An Introduction to the Creole Language

"Okay, so I guess I have to come to the realization that not everyone has been exposed to Creole culture and language. So the next few pages are for you. This should help you read through the cookbook a little easier, it should also help you understand and appreciate our culture a tad more. Here is a brief Creole vocabulary lesson for you."

~Ursula Rochon

Bonju – Hello/ Good Morning
Konmen lé-z'affè- How are things?
Konmen to yê? - How are you doing?
C'est bon, mèsi. - I'm good thanks
Wa toi pli tar. - See you later
Mo laime toi- I love you
Bonswa. - Good Evening/ Good Night

Andouille and Boudin (ahn-doo-ee and boo dan)
Two types of Cajun sausage. Andouille is made with pork, boudin with pork and rice. Sociologists recognize two major categories of Cajuns' the "River (for andouille) Cajuns" and the "Bayou (for boudin)

Beignet (bin-yay)
A fritter or strangely shaped doughnut without a hole, sprinkled with powdered sugar. A New Orleans favorite

Bouquet Garni (boo-kay gar-nee)
An herb bouquet. A small cheesecloth bag containing 1 large bay leaf, teaspoon thyme, teaspoon dried basil, about 8 sprigs fresh parsley, teaspoon dried tarragon, 3 chopped green celery tops, 6 whole peppercorns and a slashed clove of garlic used in Cajun cooking.

Bouree' (boo-ray)
Popular Cajun card game, sometimes called "Cajun Bridge"

Making Groceries
A Story of Creole Cooking from a Creole Family

C'est la vie (say la vee)
"That's life"

Cafe Noir (kaf~ay nwah)
Black coffee

Cafe~au~lait (caf~ay oh~lay)
Coffee and milk or cream

Cajun Cooking
Robust, inventive cooking evolved by the Acadian settlers rooted in resourcefulness, use of available ingredients and "made do" in artful ways

Cajuns Bayou (by-you or by-yo)
A sluggish stream bigger than a creek and smaller than a river

Cher (sha)
Term of endearment or "my sweet"

Cochon de lait (coo-shon duh lay)
An event where a suckling pig is roasted over a blistering hickory fire until the inside is tender and juicy and the outside brittle as well-cooked bacon

Comme ci, Comme ca (come-se, come sah)
So-so

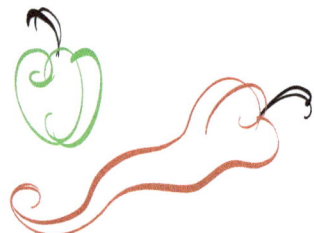

Coozan or Coozine
A term meaning cousin Cousin

Crawfish-crayfish (craw-fish)
A small fresh water crustacean related to the lobster** Etoufee (ay too fay) Method of cooking something (usually shrimp or crawfish) smothered in chopped vegetables over low flame, tightly covered until tender.

Fais-do-do (fay-doh-doh)
A type of street dance derived from European religious festivals. Originally called Festival of God.

Fleur-de-lis (fleur-de-lys); plural: fleurs-de-lis;
Meaning lily (in French, *fleur* means *flower*, and *lis* means *lily*) or iris that is used as a decorative design or symbol. It may be "at one and the same time, political, dynastic, artistic, emblematic, and symbolic", especially in heraldry.

Grillades (gree yahds)
Beef or veal round steak, browned, then simmered until tender in browned tomato sauce served over rice or grits

Making Groceries
A Story of Creole Cooking from a Creole Family

Gumbo
Thick, savory soup with chicken, seafood, sausage or okra.

Going to "Do-Do"
An expression used meaning I'm or Your going to sleep

Hush puppies
A cornbread-type of mixture, formed into balls and fried until crispy on the outside

"Ima put cha name on it"
An expression used in reference to food meaning I'll save you some.

Jambalaya
Highly-seasoned mixture of any of several combinations of seafood, meat, poultry, sausage and vegetables, simmered with raw rice until liquid is absorbed

Joie de vivre (zhwah duh viv-re)
"The joy of living" the attitude of our citizens that permeates our lifestyle

Lagniappe (lan yap)
An old Creole word for "something extra." Soup meat is the lagniappe from vegetable soup preparation

Annou derape...
(Let's get started)

Let's Cook Creole

How To's and Short Cuts...

How to make a stock...

Shrimp stock
The Shells and tails from 1 lb. of Shrimp
1/2 Cup chopped Onion
1/4 Cup chopped green onion
2 Garlic Cloves
2 Fresh Bay Leaves
1 tsp. Black Peppercorns

Add all ingredients to a 2 qt. saucepan. Cover this with cold water. Bring almost to a boil, reduce the heat to a low simmer. Simmer for about 45 minutes to an hour. Strain.

Crab Stock
The Shells and claws from 1 lb. of crab
1/2 Cup chopped Onion
1/4 Cup chopped green onion
2 Garlic Cloves
2 Fresh Bay Leaves
1 tsp. Black Peppercorns

Add all ingredients to a 2 qt. saucepan. Cover this with cold water. Bring almost to a boil, reduce the heat to a low simmer. Simmer for about 45 minutes to an hour. Strain.

Crawfish Stock
The Shells and tails from 1 lb. of crawfish
1/2 Cup chopped Onion
1/4 Cup chopped green onion
2 Garlic Cloves
2 Fresh Bay Leaves
1 tsp. Black Peppercorns

Add all ingredients to a 2 qt. saucepan. Cover this with cold water. Bring almost to a boil, reduce the heat to a low simmer. Simmer for about 45 minutes to an hour. Strain.

How To's and Short Cuts...

How to make a roux
1 cup of oil
1 cup of flour
To make a roux, simply add flour to oil, in a fry pan. For best results; use a cast iron (well-seasoned) skillet. Stir occasionally, until flour and oil are well-blended. Continue to sauté' until you have reached your desired color. The longer you stir the browner it will get(this is the flour burning) If you see black specs appear in your roux, you have to throw it out and start from scratch.

Typically this is going to be the start to any roux. Although there are different type roux's with a variance from blonde to dark brown; I prefer not to burn my oil and flour to give a darker appearance. For a brown roux I recommend you use kitchen bouquet. Which leads me to my next how-to.

How to Brown a gravy
Auntie Mimi used to always tell us to use Kitchen Bouquet to Brown a gravy, it hasn't failed yet.

How to take the bitterness out of red sauce
Add a pinch of sugar or a couple pinches until the bitterness is gone. This is for use with fresh or canned tomatoes.

How to make the dish healthier
The majority of Creole food calls for Sausage, In this day and age not everyone can handle the sodium in pork sausage, Andouille, or Boudin. When a recipe calls for sausage substitute with turkey or beef sausage; when it calls for ham, substitute with turkey ham. Tastes the exact same, you wouldn't know the difference unless I told you!

How to season and maintain your cast iron skillet
<u>Seasoning</u>: the process whereby the pores in cast iron absorb oil and create a natural non-stick finish.
Wash, (no soap), rinse, and thoroughly dry the new skillet or Dutch oven to remove the protective wax coating. Then dry your skillet over a low flame to remove all moisture from the porous metal. Put a couple tablespoons of VEGATABLE OIL in the bottom of your skillet, making sure the entire bottom is covered. Place the skillet upside down on a piece of foil and bake for 30-45 minutes at 400 degrees. Allow your newly seasoned pan to completely cool. Using a paper towel wipe out any residue, your skillet is now ready to use. Repeat this process as needed to maintain your cast iron skillet through daily use.

Cover art designed by Ursula T. Rochon

ISBN: 978-0-9965-7016-9

Library of Congress Cataloging-in-Publication Data

#2015945911

Making Groceries: A Story of Creole Cooking from a Creole Family/ URSULA T. ROCHON

1. Cook Book 2. New Orleans
3. Creole Cooking 4. Louisiana
5. Ursula T. Rochon

Printed in the United States of America

Appetizers

Crawfish Bread

2 tablespoons, plus 1 teaspoon vegetable oil
1 envelope (1/4-ounce) dry yeast
2 tablespoons
2 cups warm water (about 110 degrees F)
6 cups unbleached all-purpose flour
3/4 cup yellow cornmeal
2 teaspoons salt
1 tablespoon
1/2 cup minced onions
1 tablespoon finely chopped red bell peppers
1 tablespoon finely chopped yellow bell peppers
1 pound crawfish tails
1/4 pound grated cheddar
1/4 pound white grated cheddar cheese
Vegetable Oil for frying
Salt and pepper to taste

In the bowl of an electric mixer, place two tablespoons of the vegetable oil, yeast and sugar. The mixer should be fitted with a dough hook. Then add the water. With the mixer on low speed, beat the mixture for about 4 minutes to dissolve the yeast. *Note, if the yeast mixture doesn't begin to foam after a few minutes, it means it's not active and will have to be replaced.
In a large mixing bowl, combine the flour, 1/2 cup plus the 2 tablespoons of the cornmeal, and the salt. Then add this mixture to the yeast mixture. On low speed begin to mix the dough. Increase the speed as the dough begins to pull away from the sides of the bowl and form a ball.

Remove dough from bowl and lightly coat the entire surface with the remaining teaspoon of vegetable oil. Place dough in clean bowl (preferably glass). Cover the bowl with plastic wrap. Then set in a warm, dry place and let rise until doubled in size, about 2 hours.

Meanwhile, in a sauté pan melt the butter. Add onions and peppers. Season with salt, pepper and Creole seasoning. sauté for 2 minutes. Season crawfish with salt, pepper, and Creole seasoning and then add crawfish to the sauté pan. Sauté for 2 minutes and then remove from pan, set aside to cool to room temperature.

Crawfish Bread

When the dough has doubled in size, remove from bowl and turn onto a lightly floured surface. Using your hands gently roll dough and form a narrow loaf about 24 inches long. Now cut dough into 18 equal pieces. With a rolling pin, roll each on a lightly floured surface to form thin round disks, about 1/8-inch thick.

In a bowl combine the cooled crawfish mixture with both cheddar cheeses. Mix well.

Spread about 2 tablespoons of the filling over half of the dough round. Fold the other half of the dough over the filling, forming a half-moon shape, and then pinch the edges tightly to seal completely.

Now sprinkle two parchment lined baking sheets with remaining cornmeal. Place the completed breads on the baking sheet about 1-inch apart. Cover the breads with plastic wrap and let rise in a warm, dry place until doubled in size, about 30 minutes.

In a one gallon sauce pot, heat enough vegetable oil to freely deep fry 2 or 3 half moons at a time (several inches deep). When the oil reaches 350 degrees F carefully add the stuffed breads. Fry for about 3 minutes, turning them with a metal spoon for even frying. Remove from the oil and drain on a paper-towel lined plate. Season while hot with Creole seasoning.

Spinach Dip

My mom's version…

1 Large bag of spinach
1 onion
1 tablespoon of garlic
Breadcrumbs
Salt
Pepper
1/3 cup of butter
8oz. of cream cheese.

Sauté spinach with butter add seasonings to taste.
Place on a low fire and add cream cheese. Stir until creamy. Place spinach in an oven safe dish and place breadcrumbs on top.
Bake in oven at 350 degrees for 15 minutes or until Golden Brown.
Tip: To increase serving size add 1 bag of Spinach per every 8oz. of cream cheese and 1/3 cup of butter.

My version…

1 Large bag of spinach
1 onion
1 tablespoon of garlic
Salt to taste
Pepper to taste
1/3 cup of butter
8oz. of cream cheese.
1 large bag of mozzarella
1 large bag of provolone and parmesan

Want a little lagniappe?

To make your own breadcrumbs, take French bread and Soak the breadcrumbs overnight in butter and Creole seasoning, onion powder, garlic powder, and chopped parsley, then bake in the oven the following day and dry them out.

Sauté spinach with butter add seasonings to taste. Place on a low fire and add cream cheese. Stir until creamy. Add the mozzarella, provolone, and parmesan, until the consistency is to your liking. Place spinach in an oven safe dish and place the remainder of the cheese on top. Bake in oven at 350 degrees for 15 minutes or until Golden Brown.

Ursula's "MAN DIP"
(Named and coveted by Justin Reese)

2 lbs. of ground sirloin
4 cups of sharp cheddar cheese
12 cup of sour cream
1/2 red bell pepper
1/2 green bell pepper
1 onion
1/4 cup of garlic
1/2 cup of green onion
1 jalapeño finely diced (optional)
Creole seasoning
Whipping cream

To start, finely chop all seasoning. In a large cast iron skillet sauté, until the seasoning is fully cooked down. Add your ground meat and cook thoroughly. Add your sour cream and cheese, as your cheese is melting simultaneously add your whipping cream until you get the consistency you desire. **NOTE: this is supposed to be a dip; the more whipping cream you add the looser the dip with be. If you prefer a "meaty dip," don't be as generous with the whipping cream.** After the cheese has melted and you've reached the consistency you desire, add creole seasoning to taste and transfer into an appropriate dip dish.

Lobster and Crab Spinach Dip

1 medium red bell pepper
1 medium green bell pepper
1 cup green onion
1/2 cup parsley
1 small red onion
3 tablespoons of garlic
2 cups of crabmeat
2 cups of lobster
2 frozen bags of spinach
2 cups sharp cheddar
2 cups Italian mix cheese
1/2 cup sour cream
1 pack of cream cheese
1/2 stick butter

Chop red bell pepper, green bell pepper, garlic, parsley, green onion, red onion.

Place seasonings in large pan and Sautee until seasoning is soft, and then add lobster and shrimp. Mix for 5 minutes with butter.

Add spinach stir for another 5-10 minutes until spinach is cooked. Add sour cream and cream cheese, mix thoroughly. Add all the sharp cheddar cheese and 1 cup of the Italian cheese.

Mix until melted. Preheat oven to 350°. Place in a baking dish; add the remainder of the Italian cheese on top. Place dish in the oven and bake until golden brown.

Lump Crabmeat and Artichoke Dip

1 pound jumbo lump crabmeat
2 (8 1/2-ounce) cans artichoke hearts, drained
1/4 pound butter
1/2 cup onion, diced
1/4 cup celery, diced
1/4 cup red bell pepper, diced
1/4 cup yellow bell pepper, diced
2 tablespoons garlic, minced
1/4 tsp granulated garlic
1/4 tsp nutmeg
1/2 cup flour
2 cups chicken stock
1 pint heavy whipping cream
1 ounce dry white wine
1/4 cup green onions, sliced
1/4 cup parsley, chopped
2 cups Parmesan cheese, grated
1/2 tsp salt
1/4 tsp cayenne pepper
1/2 tsp basil, chopped

Begin by rinsing artichokes well under cold water to remove the brine. Chop artichokes coarsely in a food processor, remove and set aside for later use. In a 2-quart heavy-bottom sauté pan melt butter over medium-high heat. Add onion, celery, bell peppers and garlic. Sauté 3-5 minutes or until vegetables are wilted. Add artichokes and blend well into the vegetable mixture, stir and cook 5 additional minutes. Sprinkle in flour and blend well to form a white roux, do not brown. Add chicken stock and heavy whipping cream, one cup at a time, whisking constantly until a thick cream sauce is achieved. Reduce heat to simmer. Add white wine and season to taste using salt and pepper. Simmer approximately 15 minutes, stirring occasionally to keep from scorching. The mixture should resemble a thick cream sauce. Should it become too thick, additional whipping cream or stock may be added to reach desired consistency. Add green onions and parsley, then fold in lump crabmeat. Cook 5 minutes longer and remove from heat. Fold in Parmesan cheese and adjust seasonings if necessary. Place the mixture in a chafing dish and serve with garlic croutons or crackers.

Lump Crabmeat and Crawfish Dip

1 pound jumbo lump crabmeat
1 pound crawfish tails
¼ cup light margarine
1 cup diced onions
½ cup diced celery
¼ cup diced red bell pepper
¼ cup minced garlic
½ cup flour
3 cups evaporated skim milk
½ pound light Swiss cheese, grated
½ ounce sherry
Salt substitute to taste
Black pepper to taste
Louisiana Gold Pepper Sauce to taste

In a cast iron Dutch oven, melt margarine over medium-high heat. Add onions, celery, bell pepper and garlic. Sauté 3-5 minutes or until vegetables are wilted. Sprinkle in flour and, using a wire whisk, whip until white roux is achieved. Pour in skim milk, bring to a rolling boil and reduce to simmer. Add cheese and sherry. Continue to cook until cheese is melted. Fold in crabmeat and crawfish tails and season to taste using salt substitute, pepper and Louisiana Gold. Should you wish to recreate my great aunt's wonderful crab and cheese soup, simply add 3 cups of milk or chicken stock. Blend all ingredients well, heat and serve.

Oyster Pie

1 double pie shell
4 dozen large oysters
1 ½ tablespoons of flour
1 ½ tablespoons of butter
1 onion
½ cup celery
½ cup green onion
2 tablespoons of parsley
1 teaspoon of thyme
1 teaspoon Worchester sauce
bay leaf

Cook oysters in water until they curl.

In a separate saucepan make a roux, add celery and green onion and cook for 5 minutes. Add Oysters, parsley thyme, bay leaf and Worchester sauce. Cook over low heat. Once the sauce is creamy, add to the unbaked pie shell. Cook at 400 degrees for 40 minutes, until golden brown.

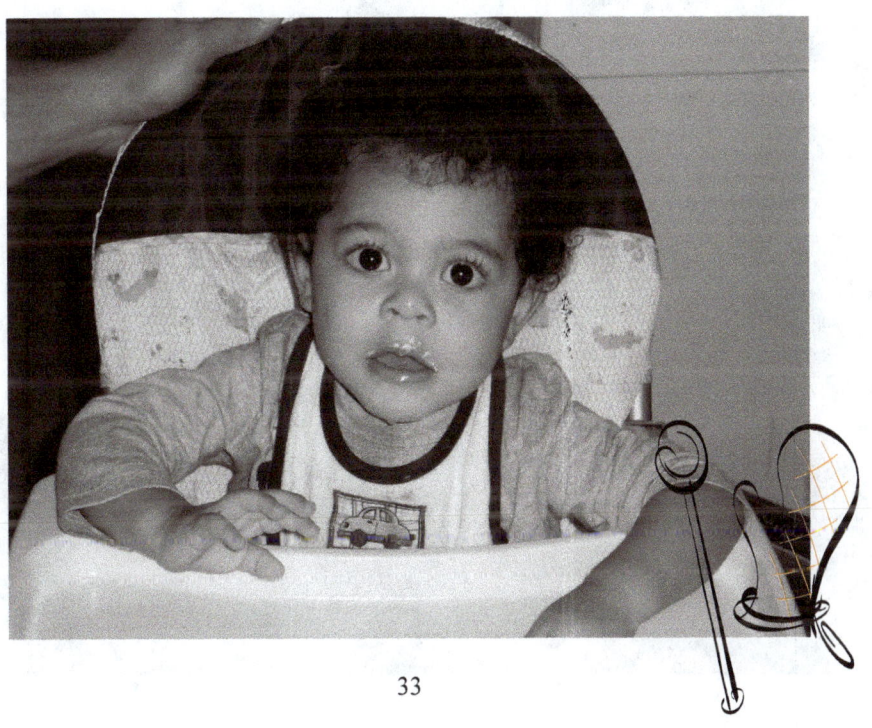

Crawfish Pies

2 sticks of butter
2 bunches of green onion
½ cup of flour
2 cans of cream of mushroom
2 lbs. of crawfish tails
2 tablespoons of white wine
4 boxes of dessert tarts (8 per box)

In a large saucepan melt butter and sauté onion. Slowly add flour and blend. After completely blended add both cans soups and stir for 5 minutes. Add crawfish, bring to medium boil again then add corn starch.
Lower heat and cook for another 10 minutes or until thick.

Grease pie shells w/butter and place pie shells in bottom of pan then add thickened mixture.

Bake at 350° for 20 minutes.

Making Groceries
A Story of Creole Cooking from a Creole Family

Hush Puppies

The phrase hush puppy is said to have come from legends dating back to the Civil War, when Southern soldiers would sit beside the campfire to prepare their dinner. When the Union soldiers would come near, they would toss their barking dogs fried cakes with the command "Hush, puppies."

2 cups yellow cornmeal
¾ cups all-purpose flour
1 teaspoon baking powder
1 teaspoon salt
1 teaspoon sugar
½ cup onion; chopped
½ cup parsley
½ cup green onion
¼ cup green bell pepper
2 cans cream style corn (16 oz)
milk, if needed
Cayenne pepper, salt and black pepper to taste
Vegetable Oil

Mix dry ingredients. Add onion, green onion, bell pepper, parsley, and corn. Mix well. If more liquid is needed to make desired consistency, add a little milk.
After desired consistency is met, then portion the mixture into balls.
In a cast iron skillet add vegetable oil, and turn heat on high. Drop the balls in and fry until golden brown.

Crab Cakes

4 lbs. Louisiana whole lump or white-select crabmeat
2 cups herbed seasoned breadcrumbs
2 extra-large egg, beaten well
1 cup real mayonnaise
1/4 cup parsley, chopped
4 Tbsp of onion minced
1/2 cup green onions, thinly sliced
1/2 tsp. salt
1 tsp. Creole Seasoning
1 tsp. black pepper
2 Tbsp. Worcestershire sauce
1 Tbsp. Dijon mustard
1 tsp. dry mustard
Cayenne pepper to taste
Margarine and butter for frying (equal amounts)

First, place the crabmeat into a deep glass bowl, sift through it to make sure all of the shell pieces have been thoroughly removed. NOTHING can ruin a good crab cake like biting into a piece of shell.

In a second bowl, mix together the breadcrumbs, egg, mayonnaise, parsley, onion, green onions, and all of the seasonings (salt, black pepper, seafood seasoning, Worcestershire, Dijon, and dry mustard).

Now it's time for you to add the crabmeat to the breadcrumb mixture. Gently mix the crabmeat thoroughly. I suggest you not use a spoon or an electric mixer otherwise you will break up the large lumps of crab meat. If the texture appears to be too dry you can add a little more mayonnaise.

Now lightly flour your hands and create a patty into the shape of a 3-inch crab cakes. Then, using just enough butter or margarine to prevent sticking, cook the cakes in a frying pan until they are toasty brown (it will take about 5 minutes on each side).

Crab Corn Soup

1/2 cup butter
1 cup onion, chopped
1/2 cup green onion
1/2 cup of parsley chopped
6 cups of crab stock
2 tablespoons of garlic
2 bay leaves
1/2 teaspoon cayenne pepper
1 teaspoon Cajun seasoning
salt and pepper to taste
2 14oz. Cans of whole kernel corn
1/2 cup half-and-half
3 tablespoons all-purpose flour
1/2 cup milk
24 ounces fresh lump crab-meat

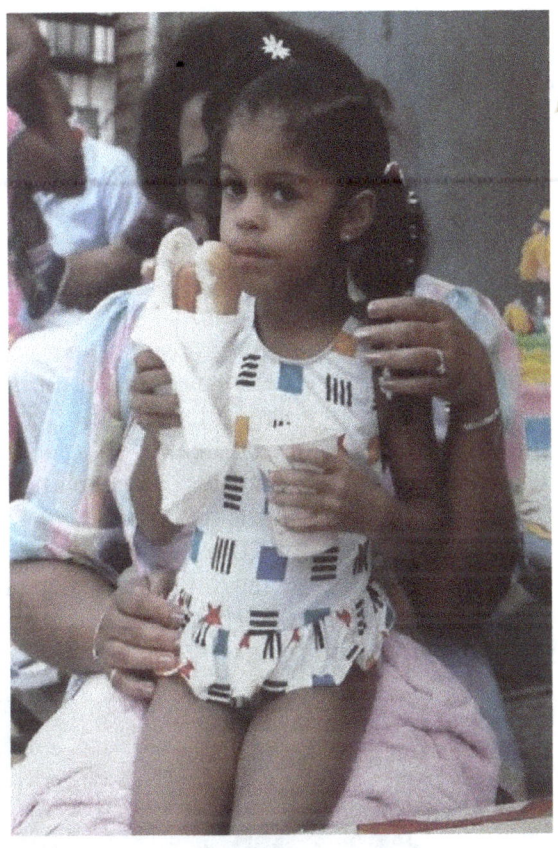

Heat butter in a large pot over medium heat. Stir in onion; cook until soft and translucent. Now add your green onion and parsley, and bring to a boil. Stir in garlic, bay leaves, cayenne pepper, Cajun seasoning, salt, and pepper. Stir corn into boiling broth. Simmer about 10 minutes. Reduce heat to medium low.

Now you are going to thicken your soup... remove 1 cup of soup, and let it cool slightly. Pour your soup into a food processor and add your half-and-half blend thoroughly for 30 to 45 seconds.

In a separate bowl stir your flour and milk, slowly stir into the soup. Stirring constantly, simmer for 1 to 2 minutes. Now stir in pureed mixture. Reduce heat to low, stir in crab meat, and cook until warmed through, about 5 minutes.

Corn Pudding

1/2 cup sugar
1 stick of butter, melted
1 can whole kernel corn
1 can of cream corn
1 large egg
1 cups milk
2 tablespoons vanilla
2 tablespoons cup cinnamon

In a lightly buttered casserole dish, combine sugar; butter, vanilla and cinnamon. Mix in corn and melted butter. Beat egg and add to milk. Stir into the corn mixture. Preheat oven to 450°.
Place in oven for 10 minutes. Remove and stir with long prong fork, disturbing the top as little as possible.
Return to the oven for 10 more minutes. Repeat stirring procedure.
Return to oven for 10 more minutes. Repeat stirring procedure.
Return to oven for 10 - 15 minutes. Top should be lightly brown and pudding should be firm.

Making Groceries
A Story of Creole Cooking from a Creole Family

Making Groceries
A Story of Creole Cooking from a Creole Family

Sides

Jambalaya

2 large Onion
1 ½ cup of Green onion
1 cup bell pepper
1 cup Parsley
2 cans Tomato Paste
2 large cans tomato Sauce
1 cans whole tomatoes
6 ounces Turkey Sausage
6 ounces Beef Sausage
3 lbs. of shrimp
Rice

Finely chop all vegetables.

Brown your meat on each side using medium-high heat. Then add your onion and bell pepper to sauté' with the meat. After vegetables are slightly tender, turn fire on low and set aside. Sauté onions, garlic, bell pepper, parsley, and tomato paste. After completely sautéed add tomato sauce.

In a separate pan sauté the rest of your vegetables, with your tomato paste. Once slightly tender add the sausage, onion, and bell pepper into the mixture. Turn on low and let simmer. Add your tomato sauce let it simmer.

After about 10 minutes add a small amount of water and let simmer for about 10 additional minutes. This is a good time to add your shrimp.

Lower heat and add rice; stir often until rice is fully cooked.

Jambalaya tip: For you first timers out there; I recommend cooking the rice FIRST and then add it into the jambalaya sauce and mix it together.

Okay I just as soon tell you that the first time I attempted to cook the un-cooked rice in the jambalaya sauce, I made a mess. Half of the rice was crunchy the other half was soggy. I was not happy. I think the only reason my husband ate it any was because he didn't want to see me throw all the sausage and shrimp away.

Jambalaya Pasta

Take the same recipe and substitute pasta in place of your rice. Cook the pasta a dente' in a separate pot, drain, and then mix the tomato mixture. Enjoy!

Mimi's Potato Salad

2 lbs of potatoes
6 eggs
Green onion
1/2 cup of parsley
1 cup of celery
1/4 cup green Bell pepper
1/4 cup red Bell pepper
Salt
Pepper
Garlic powder
Onion powder
Cayenne pepper
Creole seasoning
Mayonnaise
Mustard
Paprika to garnish

Place your potatoes and eggs in a large pot of water, and bring to boil. Cook thoroughly.

After cooking peel potatoes and eggs and place in a large mixing bowl, and set aside. Finely chop parsley, green onion, celery, and bell pepper. Add your chopped seasoning to the bowl of potatoes and eggs.

Use your mixing spoon to break up the potatoes and eggs. There is no need to chop them, before putting them in the bowl. Mix contents until even. Now add your garlic, onion powder, creole seasoning, and cayenne pepper, mix thoroughly. Add mayonnaise and mustard to desire consistency.

It's better to add a little mayonnaise at a time, you can always add more if needed.

TIP: Use room temperature mayonnaise, if you use mayonnaise that has been refrigerated there is a greater chance that your potato salad will "separate."

After contents are fully mixed and you have achieved your desired flavor, transfer to a serving dish and garnish with Paprika

Sweet Potatoes

6 lbs sweet potatoes
1 tablespoons pure cane syrup
1/3 cup sweetened condensed milk
1 lb butter, softened
2 tablespoons brown sugar (dark or light)
1 whole orange, juiced (or 1/2 cup orange juice)
1/2 teaspoons cinnamon
1/2 teaspoons sugar
1 pinch ground nutmeg
1 cup raisins (optional)
2 cups chopped pecans
8 oz pralines, broken into pieces (about 8 whole pralines)

Bake the sweet potatoes at 350 degrees until fork tender.

Remove the skin and place the cooked potatoes into a mixing bowl with syrup, condensed milk, butter, & brown sugar. Start beating with a paddle mixer and gradually add the orange juice, lemon zest, & lemon juice until the mixture is smooth.

Then, gently fold in the nutmeg, cinnamon, sugar, raisins, pecans, & pralines. Transfer mixture to a glass casserole dish and bake at 350 degrees for approximately 20 minutes.

For an extra bonus, you can top with a meringue and return to the oven, baking until golden brown. If not, you can simply top with whipped cream & sprinkle with some more cinnamon, sugar, & nutmeg. Mmmm...Mmmm. Delicious.

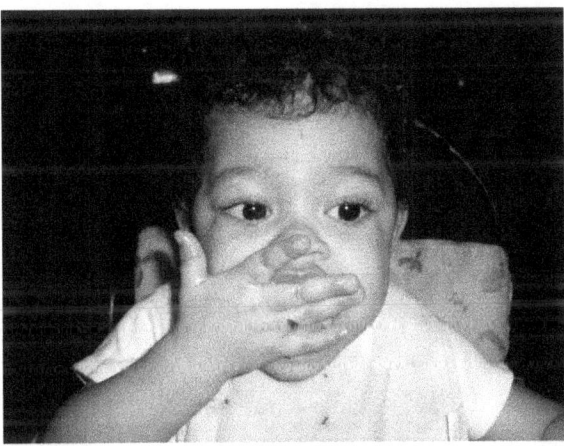

Auntie Mimi's Candied Yams in Orange Cups

6 pounds large yams
1/2 cup marshmallow crème
9 tablespoons butter, room temperature
6 tablespoons brown sugar
6 tablespoons of condensed milk
1 teaspoon of nutmeg
1 teaspoon of cinnamon
3 large eggs
9 large oranges
Additional marshmallow crème for garnish
36 pecan halves for garnish
Maraschino Cherries for garnish

Thoroughly wash each yam, dry, and puncture with a fork all over. Preheat oven to 350°F, place on a non stick baking tray and bake in oven for an hour on 350°F or until tender. (This process can be done the night before, just make sure to refrigerate the yams overnight)

Add 3/4 cup marshmallow crème, butter, brown sugar, condensed milk, nutmeg, and cinnamon; mash until smooth. Whisk in eggs.

Preheat oven to 350°F. Cut thin slice from top and bottom of each orange to make flat surfaces. Cut oranges in half. Scoop out pulp; reserve for another use. Place orange cups on 2 baking sheets. Divide yam mixture equally among cups. Top each with dollop of marshmallow crème and 2 pecan halves.

Bake until beginning to brown, about 30 minutes.

Baked Green Beans

2 cans of cream of mushroom soup
1 cup of milk
2 teaspoons soy sauce
1/4 teaspoon black pepper
8 cups of cooked green beans
1 can 6 ounce French Fried Onions
1/4 teaspoon to taste

In a large mixing bowl stir cream of mushroom soup, milk, soy sauce, black pepper, and green beans. Place green beans mixture in a large sauce pan and stir until warm. Season with black pepper and salt. After the mixture is hot, place in a large baking pan. Cover green bean casserole with foil.

Pre-heat oven to 350 degrees.

Bake green bean casserole at 350 degrees covered for 25 minutes. After casserole is fully cooked uncover and let cook for 5 additional minutes or until golden brown.

Mom's Stuffed Bell Peppers

6 large bell peppers
2 tablespoons butter
1 cup chopped onions
2 stalks of celery
½ cup parsley
2 large cloves of garlic
2 lbs of ground beef
2 lbs of shrimp, cleaned
3 cups of bread crumb stuffing mix
3 eggs, slightly beaten
1 teaspoon salt
1 teaspoon Creole seasoning
1 teaspoon of black pepper or cayenne pepper
1 can of beef broth
or chicken broth

Cut bell peppers in half. Remove stems and seeds from bell pepper, and put then in a baking pan. Set this aside for later.

After all of your seasonings have been finely chopped set them aside.

Melt the butter in a cast iron skillet over a medium low heat. Add your seasonings to the skillet and begin to sauté'. After the vegetables are slightly tender, add your ground beef, sauté, until lightly browned. Then add your stuffing mix and your Creole seasoning, salt, and pepper to taste. Now add your shrimp. Once the shrimp are cooked, remove from fire and let cool slightly. Work the eggs into the stuffing. If more moisture is needed add your chicken broth. Spoon the stuffing into the prepared bell peppers and place them in a shallow baking dish.

Bake at 305 degrees for 30 minutes or until the bell peppers are tender.

Stuffed Mirliton

6 Mirlitons, sliced lengthwise
1 pound jumbo lump crabmeat
1 pound medium shrimp, peeled and deveined
1 pound ground beef
¼ pound butter
2 cup diced onions
2 cup diced green onion
1 cup diced bell peppers
1/2 cup minced garlic
Creole Seasoning, to taste
1/2 cup chopped parsley
3 eggs
2 cups Italian bread crumbs
12 pats butter

Preheat oven to 375°F. Boil sliced mirlitons in lightly-salted water 30–40 minutes or until inside/meat is tender enough to scoop from shells. Once tender, remove from water and cool. Using a teaspoon, remove seeds and gently scoop all insides/meat out of shell, being careful not to tear shell. Discard excess liquid accumulated while scooping insides/meat out.

Reserve meat and save shells for stuffing. In a 12-inch cast iron skillet, melt butter over medium-high heat. Sauté onions, green onion, bell peppers, garlic, ground beef, and Creole Seasoning until vegetables are wilted and ground beef is completely cooked. Blend in shrimp and cook 2–3 minutes or until pink and curled. Mix in reserved meat from mirlitons, and parsley.

Cook for an additional 15–20 minutes, stirring until well blended, don't over-cooked or your shrimp will become chewy. After most of liquid has evaporated, remove from heat and season with salt, and pepper. Sprinkle in approximately 1½ cups of bread crumbs and eggs to absorb any excess liquid and to hold stuffing intact.

Fold in crabmeat, being careful to not break lumps. Divide mixture into 12 equal portions and stuff into hollowed-out shells. Place stuffed mirlitons on baking pan and sprinkle with remaining bread crumbs.

Top each Mirliton with 1 pat of butter. Bake 30 minutes or until golden brown. Serve 1 Mirliton half as a vegetable or 2 halves as an entrée.

Theresa's Baked Macaroni

2 (12 ounce) package macaroni
3 eggs
1 cup heavy whipping cream
1 stick of butter, melted
2 1/2 cups shredded Cheddar cheese
salt and pepper to taste
Creole seasoning to taste
1 tablespoon onion powder
1 tablespoon garlic powder
1/4 cup of parsley

Preheat the oven to 350 degrees F (175 degrees C). Lightly grease a 2-quart baking dish.

In a large pot of salted water, lightly boil the macaroni for about 5 minutes until cooked al dente'. Drain pasta and place back in pot on low heat, add butter and stir. In a separate bowl whisk the eggs, and heavy cream together in a large cup, then pour mixture in pasta. Continue stirring and add cheese, and garlic, onion, and Creole seasoning powder. Add parsley, save some for garnish.

Place the lightly cooked macaroni in the prepared baking dish. Press the mixture evenly around the baking dish. Sprinkle the remainder of the parsley for garnish on top. Cover with foil. Bake covered, for 20 to 30 minutes, towards the last 15 minutes uncover and let brown.

Ursula's Shrimp Pasta

2lbs. shrimp
2 12 ounce bags of pasta
1 medium red bell pepper
1 medium green pepper
1 cup green onion
2 tablespoons of garlic
2 cups heavy whipping cream
3 cups sharp cheddar cheese
1 teaspoon olive oil
creole seasoning to taste

Chop all seasoning and set aside.

Thoroughly boil pasta until al dente and drain, and set aside.

In a large skillet, add olive oil and chopped seasoning.

Sauté seasoning until tender. Add shrimp and continue to stir until shrimp are cooked, add whipping cream and mix thoroughly.

Add pasta and stir until blended

Add cheese and stir until fully blended.

Serve with toasted/buttered French bread.

Grillades
(Best when served traditionally with grits)

2 lbs Round Steak
2 teaspoons Salt
¼ teaspoon cayenne Pepper
½ Cup Flour seasoned
2 Tablespoons Creole Seasoning
3 Tablespoons Vegetable Oil
3 Tablespoons Butter
2 Medium Onions
1 Red Bell Pepper
4 Ribs Celery
1/4 cup Garlic
2 Cups Beef Stock
3 Tbsp Homemade Worcestershire Sauce
2 Cups Tomatoes, Chopped
2 Fresh Bay Leaves
1 Tablespoons Red Wine Vinegar
1 Tablespoon Corn Starch (whisked together with 1 Tablespoon Water)
1/2 cup Flat Leaf Parsley, chopped
1 cup Green Onions, thinly sliced on the bias
Salt & Pepper to taste
1 Recipe of Grits made according to the Package Instructions

Pound the Round Steak on both sides to about ½ inch thickness, then cut into pieces and season with salt and pepper. In a separate bowl combine the flour and Creole Seasoning, dip the pieces in one at a time, shaking off any excess. In a cast iron pot, heat the vegetable oil over medium fire until hot, now brown the steak well on both sides without burning. After the meat is brown on each side, drain meat on a plate, and set aside.

Now melt the butter over medium heat and sauté' your onions, Bell Pepper, Celery, and Garlic. You want your vegetables to be soft but not too brown. Stir in the Beef Stock, Worcestershire, Tomatoes, and Bay Leaves; add parsley and green onion and bring the mixture to a boil.

Reduce the heat to medium-low. Add the steak, and any of the drippings to the pot. Submerge the steak in the sauce and simmer for about 1 ½ hours or until they're very tender. When the steak (Grillades) are tender remove them to a plate and bring the sauce to a boil. Add the corn starch mixture and whisk until the sauce is slightly thickened. Stir in the red wine vinegar, hot sauce, and salt & pepper. Serve with your favorite side.

Cowan
(Turtle Soup)

3 onions
6 stalks of celery
1 cup vegetable oil
Peel from one lemon
1/2 cup Worcestershire sauce
1/4 cup Crystal Hot Sauce (much less if you use Tabasco Brand)
4 large fresh tomatoes
3 chopped green onions
salt and pepper to taste
3 chopped green bell peppers
3 clove garlic, chopped
1 tablespoons oregano
1 cup dry sherry
2 lb turtle meat

Boil two pounds of boneless turtle meat in two quarts of water for an hour and a half. Take out meat and reserve stock. Chop turtle meat into half-inch cubes. It will probably shred up. That is good. Chop onions, celery, peppers, and garlic. Bring oil to heat in a nice, thick pot at least eight quarts. Cook down the seasoning until it is very, very soft, stirring often. Add basil and oregano. Add flour slowly, cooking this roux for a few minutes. Add diced tomatoes, hot sauce, Worcestershire, sherry and turtle stock, stirring constantly. Add turtle meat and the chopped peel of the lemon, when this thick mixture comes to heat add at least another quart or two of water to thin out the mixture.

After this boils slowly for 30 minutes, add coarse chopped egg and green onions and parsley. Add salt and pepper.

If you can get fresh turtle meat this soup is out of this world. If y'all come to town and stay with us we'll check the market around the corner and if they have live Cowan they can strip out the meat, pack it and ship it to you.

Family and Friends

Mama Gourrier's Seafood Pasta Salad

This was passed on to me from my mother from her mother.
Assunta Gourrier-Jackson

1 lbs Box of Elbow Pasta
2 lbs of Shrimp , cleaned
1 16oz. Container of
White Crab Meat or Claws
1 quart of Dukes or Blue Plate Mayo
1 8 oz bag of Shredded Cheddar Cheese
1 cup of green onion
1/2 teaspoon of Cayenne Pepper
1/2 teaspoon of Black Pepper
1 Grated Lemon Rime
Salt to taste

Assunta Jackson & her mother
Edna Gourrier

Night before: Place shrimp with little water in sauce pan with Old Bay or New Orleans crab boil and chill .

Boil your pasta as well, after cooked chill in refrigerator. This process will cut your time in half as you won't have to wait for the pasta to cool.

In large mixing bowl place your elbow pasta, and chopped green onion. Mix in grated lemon rime, cayenne pepper salt and pepper. Next add cheese, chilled shrimp and crabmeat or claws, take a whole quart of Mayo and mix well. Garnish with parsley or lettuce with lemon. Cover and chill in refrigerator, until ready to serve.

Gourrier tip: You should prepare this the night before, it gives the seasoning time to marinate, giving your pasta salad that really flavorful taste when time to serve.

Edna Gourrier's Pasta Salad

The Gourrier Family

Assunta Gourrier's Yakamein

1 box of spaghetti pasta
1 jar beef bouillon
1/2 cup of green onions
3 seasoned steaks, cubed
2 tablespoons of soy sauce
12 cups water
4 boiled eggs {optional}

In a large stock pot add 12 cups of water, then add 25 beef bouillon cubes and bring to boil.

Add beef cubes, 1/4 cups of green onion (save the other 1/4 for garnish) and pasta and reduce heat.

Add soy sauce and let simmer for 25 to 30 minutes.

Add boiled eggs and garnish with green onion per serving.

You can replace the beef, with seasoned pork chops, shrimp, or chicken.

Ursula's famous Super Bowl Wings

20-25 chicken wings
1/2 cup minced onion
1 cup chopped green onion
1/4 cup minced garlic
1/2 cup of parsley
Mesquite Marinade
1 teaspoon of lime
To taste:
    Salt
    Pepper
    Creole Seasoning
    Cayenne

Marinate wings overnight in Mesquite Marinade sauce.

In a crock-pot:

Place wings in crock-pot, with onions, green onion , garlic, and teaspoon of lime. Add seasonings to taste. Cover crock-pot and cook on low heat for 4-5 hours.

In a baking pan:

In a large bowl season chicken thoroughly. Toss the chicken with onion powder, garlic powder, salt, pepper, cayenne pepper, Creole seasoning, and parsley flakes, and lime.

Layer wings in baking pan with onions, green onion, and garlic in-between. Cover the baking sheet with foil.

Pre-heat the oven to 325 degrees. Place chicken in oven and bake for 3 hours. After cooked, remove foil and let brown for 15 minutes.

Enjoy!

Making Groceries
A Story of Creole Cooking from a Creole Family

Rochon Seafood Gumbo

1/2 cup oil
1/2 cup flour
2 large onions, diced
½ green bell peppers, diced
4-6 cloves garlic, minced
4 quarts shrimp stock, crab stock or fish stock
1 tablespoon Creole seasoning blend
2 bay leaves
6 Ounces of turkey sausage
File', Cayenne pepper, salt and black pepper to taste
2 pounds medium shrimp, peeled and de-veined
2 dozen oysters, freshly shucked, liquor reserved
4 blue crabs, cleaned (optional)
1 pound fresh lump crabmeat, picked over for shells and cartilage
1 tablespoon filé powder
8 cups cooked long-grain white rice

Cut the turkey sausage into 1-inch pieces. Chop all of your seasonings and set aside for later. In a large saucepan or Cast Iron pot, heat the vegetable oil over medium heat. Tilt the pan so that it coats the bottom and add the sausage. Cover and cook, turning occasionally, for 3 minutes, until lightly browned.

What am I going to tell you to do now…Make a ROUX!
After your roux is brown, then add the onions, bell pepper, parsley, green onion, and garlic. Sauté the seasonings for about 10 minutes or until vegetables are tender.

Add the seasonings, (Vibration cooking time) salt, cayenne, pepper, and black pepper. Now add the stock, or chicken broth. Bring to a boil, and then reduce heat to simmer and cook another 30 minutes.
Add whole blue crabs. Remove the hard top shell from the crabs (do not throw AWAY we are going to use these later) and break each crab in two down the middle. Remove the claws. Add to the stock.) With the gumbo on very low heat, add the shrimp 10 minutes before serving, the oysters and oyster liquor 5 minutes before serving, and the crabmeat just before serving (don't cook the crabmeat, just stir until it is heated through).
Remove from heat and sprinkle the filé powder on the surface of the gumbo, then cover and let stand for 15 minutes.
Place rice in each bowl and ladle the gumbo over and around it.

Making Groceries
A Story of Creole Cooking from a Creole Family

Turkey Sausage Gumbo

6 ounces Andouille
6 ounces of turkey sausage
2lbs. of shrimp
2 large onions
1 bunch of green onion
¼ of medium green pepper
1 bunch of parsley
2 large garlic clove
4 cans (14 1/2 ounces) chicken broth or turkey stock*
File', Cayenne pepper, salt and black pepper to taste
Creole Seasoning to taste
8 cups cooked long-grain white rice

Cut the turkey sausage into 1-inch pieces. Chop all of your seasonings and set aside for later. In a large saucepan or Cast Iron pot, heat the vegetable oil over medium heat. Tilt the pan so that it coats the bottom and add the sausage. Cover and cook, turning occasionally, for 3 minutes, until lightly browned.

In a large stock pot fill with chicken broth or turkey stock, cover and bring to a boil. In a separate saucepan, begin cooking your roux*. Once the roux is browned add that to the stock pot, stir until fully blended. If your gumbo begins to look to thick add another can of chicken broth (this is your introduction to vibration cooking)

This is the order in which you add your ingredients.....If you decide to add in the order you wish, that's your prerogative, but please don't call me when you end up with a pot full of mess.

After you have added the roux to the chicken broth or stock, add your seasonings. After you have added your seasonings, then add your already browned sausage. Always add your seafood last. Nobody likes gummy overcooked shrimp.

Reduce the heat to low and simmer, stirring often, for 3 to 5 minutes or until the vegetables are tender and the gumbo has thickened slightly. Season to taste with cayenne, salt, and pepper and don't forget the file'

Cook rice in a separate pot, or rice cooker if that's easier. Ladle the gumbo into 4 large soup bowls and serve.

* Please read the how to section about making roux.

Okra Gumbo

2 pounds fresh or frozen shrimp, head on about 40-50 count per pound
3 quarts water
2 Tablespoons cooking oil
1 quart fresh or frozen okra, sliced into _" rounds
2/3 cup cooking oil
1/2 cup all purpose flour
2 cups chopped onions
1 cup chopped green bell pepper
1/2 cup chopped celery
1 teaspoon garlic, finely chopped
1 16oz. can chopped tomatoes
2 bay leaves
2 teaspoons salt, or to taste
1/2 teaspoon black pepper (or to taste)
1/2 teaspoon white pepper (or to taste)
1/4 teaspoon cayenne pepper (or to taste)

Peel and de-vein the shrimp, and set aside, covered in the refrigerator. Save the shrimp heads and use them to make your stock. (forgot?? Check the how to's in the front of the book.) Strain, discard the shells and heads and set the stock aside.

In a heavy bottomed skillet, heat 2 tablespoons of oil, add the okra and sauté over medium high heat for about 10 - 15 minutes or until all the "ropiness" is gone. This step may take a little longer if fresh okra is used. Place the cup oil in a large (8 quart) heavy bottomed Dutch oven type pot. Make a dark brown roux. When you have achieved the desired color, add the onions, bell pepper, celery and garlic; Sauté until tender. During this process, allow the vegetables to stick to the bottom of the pan a bit, then scrape the bottom with a metal spoon or spatula. This allows some of the natural sugars in the onions to caramelize, rendering great depth of flavor.

When the seasoning vegetables are tender add the tomatoes, bay leaves and the three peppers and a little salt. Cook for about 10 minutes, repeating the stick and scrape process with the tomatoes. Add the sautéed okra and cook for 10 more minutes. Add the crab stock and half of the shrimp stock to the pot. Stirring constantly, bring the pot to a boil. Lower the heat a bit, partially cover and simmer for thirty minutes, stirring occasionally. If the gumbo appears too thick, add more stock to adjust. Add salt to taste and adjust the pepper if desired. Add the broken crabs and simmer for about 10 minutes. Add the peeled shrimp, return to a boil and simmer until the shrimp are firm and pink, about 5 minutes. Remove the pot from heat.

Gumbo Z'Herbes

For the greens:
5 bunches greens, such as collard greens, chicory, dandelion greens, mustard greens, spinach, parsley, beet tops, carrot tops, or turnip tops (enough to equal about 3 pounds)
3 cups water

For the gumbo base:
2/3 cup vegetable oil
2/3 cup all-purpose flour
1 medium yellow onion, medium dice
1 bunch scallions, white and light green parts thinly sliced, green tops reserved for garnish
1 large green bell pepper, medium dice
4 stalks celery, medium dice
1 large garlic clove, minced (about 2 teaspoons)
2 cups water or low-sodium vegetable broth
2 teaspoons kosher salt
2 tablespoons Cajun seasoning (either purchased or homemade)
2 whole cloves
3 allspice berries
2 dried bay leaves
1 tablespoon minced marjoram leaves
Green Tabasco

Rinse and trim greens, removing any dried-out parts or tough stems that don't break easily. If you are using collards, remove the tough inner rib that runs up the center of each leaf.

Fill the sink with cold water and submerge all greens. Leave undisturbed for about 5 minutes, then lift from the water and place in a colander. (Don't drain the sink with the greens still in it: Soaking the greens allows all the sand and grit to settle to the bottom of the sink—if you drain it, your greens are left sitting in the salty stuff.) If necessary, repeat this process.

Chop or tear greens into large pieces and place in a large saucepan or pot with a tight fitting lid. Add water to greens and season generously with salt; place over medium-high heat. When the water in the pot begins to simmer, tightly cover and reduce heat to medium low. Cook greens, occasionally turning with a pair of tongs, until they are very soft and wilted, about 15 to 20 minutes.

Gumbo Z'Herbes
(continued)

Strain greens, being sure to reserve the cooking liquid. (You should have about 3 1/2 cups.) Allow greens to cool slightly, then chop into 1/2-inch pieces. Take about 1/2 of the chopped greens and purée them in a food processor or blender (if greens will not blend, add a little of the reserved cooking liquid to help them along).

In a large, heavy pot or Dutch oven, heat vegetable oil over medium heat. When it is hot, slowly sprinkle in flour, stirring constantly with a wire whisk to prevent any lumps from forming. Reduce heat to medium low and cook roux, stirring constantly (and taking care to scrape out the corners of the pan), until it is a nutty brown color (the color of peanut butter) and emits a toasted aroma, about 10 to 15 minutes.

Use a wooden spoon to stir onion, scallions, bell pepper, celery, and garlic into the pot. Season with a pinch of salt and freshly ground black pepper. Cook, stirring often, until vegetables are softened and garlic is no longer raw-smelling, about 5 minutes.

Add reserved cooking liquid along with vegetable broth or water, stirring well to incorporate. Increase heat to medium high and bring mixture to a simmer. Stir in salt, Cajun seasoning, cloves, allspice, and bay leaves and simmer, stirring often, until gumbo base is soupy and thick and vegetables are tender, about 15 minutes.

Stir in chopped and puréed greens and marjoram; cover the pot and simmer 10 minutes.

Add Tabasco to taste and serve over cooked white rice, garnished with thinly sliced scallion tops.

White Beans

2 large onions
½ cup of parsley
2 bunches of green onion
1 clove of garlic
1/2 cup green bell pepper
12 ounces of sausage
1 quart (4 cups) dried white beans
2 quarts water
4 smoked turkey necks

In a large pot bring your white beans, turkey necks and onions to a boil. Once your onions appear transparent add garlic, green onion, parley, and bell pepper. Continue to stir. In a separate pan fry your sausage. Fry both sides until olden brown. When the beans are close to being finished (the broth looks creamy and soupy), add your sausage.

Sausage tip: Make sure the sausage is brown on both sides; otherwise it will get soggy once it's sits in the beans.

Once the beans are almost done, remove a spoonful of the white beans and smash them in a cup. Add gravy as you smash the beans. Once the beans a fully smashed and mixed with the gravy you have removed from the stock pot return it back to the pot. This will make them creamy. YUM!

Red Beans and Rice

2 large onions
½ cup of parsley
2 bunches of green onion
1 clove of garlic
1/2 cup of green bell pepper
12 ounces of sausage
1 quart (4 cups) dried red beans
2 quarts water
1 pound ham or salt pork
1 carrot, chopped
1 large onion, chopped

Pepper, salt, cayenne pepper, and Creole seasoning to taste

In a large stock pot bring water to a boil. Cut Onions in quarters and drop tem in. Yes, I said it, drop them in. They don't have to be cut fine, so why waste your time doing so.

In a separate frying pan sauté green onion, garlic, and parsley; add this to the boiling water and onions. At this point you should add your red beans to the boiling water.

In the same pan brown your sausage. To give the sausage a good flavor, leave some of the sautéed seasoning in the frying pan, once the sausage is brown, add it to the beans.

Sausage tip: Make sure the sausage is brown on both sides; otherwise it will get soggy once it's sits in the beans.

Once the beans are almost done, remove a spoonful of the red beans and smash them in a cup. Add gravy as you smash the beans. Once the beans a fully smashed and mixed with the gravy you have removed from the stock pot return it back to the pot. This will make them creamy. YUM!

Shrimp Étouffée'

4 Tbsp plus 1 tsp Creole Seasoning
8 Tbsp Vegetable Oil
3/8 Cup All purpose Flour
1/2 Cup Onion, Finely Chopped
1/2 Cup Celery, Finely Chopped
1/2 Cup Bell Pepper, Finely Chopped
4 Tbsp Minced Garlic
3 Cups Shrimp Stock (Please refer to How to's of Creole Cooking)
2 Sticks of Butter
1 Cup Green Onions, thinly sliced
2 lb Good Quality Shrimp, Peeled and Deveined,
Salt & Freshly Ground Black Pepper to taste

While your stock is simmering heat the oil over medium heat. Add the flour and stir to make a Roux 7-10 minutes. Remove the pan from the heat and stir in 2 Tablespoons of the seasoning, Onions, Celery, Bell Pepper, and the Garlic. Set aside.

When the stock is finished and strained, bring 1 cup of it to a boil. Whisk the Roux and vegetable mixture in and reduce the heat to a simmer. Simmer for 5 minutes

In a large Cast-Iron frying pan, melt the butter over medium heat. Add the Green Onions, Shrimp, and remaining 2 tsp Creole Seasoning. Sauté until the Shrimp just starts to turn pink. Add 1/2 Cup more of the Shrimp Stock and the remaining butter; cook until the butter is melted and incorporated into the sauce, 3-5 minutes, constantly shaking the pan back-and-forth (versus stirring). If you sauce starts to separate, add a splash of stock and continue shaking the pan.

Crawfish Étouffée'

4 Tbsp plus 1 tsp Creole Seasoning
8 Tbsp Vegetable Oil
3/8 Cup All purpose Flour
1/2 Cup Onion, Finely Chopped
1/2 Cup Celery, Finely Chopped
1/2 Cup Bell Pepper, Finely Chopped
4 Tbsp Minced Garlic
3 Cups Crawfish Stock (Please refer to How to's of Creole Cooking)
2 Sticks of Butter
1 Cup Green Onions, thinly sliced
2 lb crawfish tails, fresh or frozen
Salt & Freshly Ground Black Pepper to taste

While your stock is simmering heat the oil over medium heat. Add the flour and stir to make a Roux 7-10 minutes. Remove the pan from the heat and stir in 2 Tablespoons of the seasoning, Onions, Celery, Bell Pepper, and the Garlic. Set aside.

When the stock is finished and strained, bring 1 cup of it to a boil. Whisk the Roux and vegetable mixture in and reduce the heat to a simmer. Simmer for 5 minutes.

In a large Cast-Iron frying pan, melt the butter over medium heat. Add the Green Onions, Crawfish, and remaining 2 tsp Creole Seasoning. Sauté until the Crawfish just starts to turn pink. Add 1/2 Cup more of the Crawfish Stock and the remaining butter; cook until the butter is melted and incorporated into the sauce, 3-5 minutes, constantly shaking the pan back-and-forth (versus stirring). If you sauce starts to separate, add a splash of stock and continue shaking the pan. Serve traditionally over rice.

Crawfish Bisque
(Next 3 pages)

Stuffed crawfish heads:

1/4 cup oil
1/2 cup flour
2 medium onions, finely minced
1 large bell pepper, finely minced
3/4 cup stock or water
2 teaspoons salt
Freshly ground black pepper
1-1/2 teaspoons cayenne pepper
2 large eggs, well beaten
2 cups plain French bread crumbs
1/4 cup chopped parsley
1/4 cup minced green onions with tops
4 tablespoons butter, melted
5 dozen cleaned crawfish heads
Flour for dusting

Make a roux with the oil and flour. Add onions and bell peppers and cook until tender, stirring constantly. Mince or grind the remaining half of the crawfish tails and add to the roux-onion mixture. Add the remaining crawfish fat and simmer for 15 minutes.

Add stock, salt, peppers, breadcrumbs, eggs, parsley, green onions and butter. Combine thoroughly, adjusting the consistency with more stock or more bread crumbs as needed.

Fill each head with stuffing. Roll in flour and bake at 350°F for 15 minutes, or fry in hot oil until the stuffing is golden brown.

Crawfish Bisque

20 pounds live crawfish
4 packets Zatarain's Crab, Shrimp and Crawfish Boil seasoning
3 lemons, quartered
6 tablespoons butter
1/2 cup peanut oil
1 cup flour
2 large onions, finely minced
1 large bell pepper, finely minced
3 ribs celery, finely minced
4 cloves garlic, finely minced
5 cups shellfish stock or water
1 tablespoon salt, or to taste
Freshly ground black pepper, to taste
1 tablespoon Creole seasoning
2 teaspoons cayenne pepper
2 teaspoons thyme
1/2 cup chopped green onion tops
1/2 cup chopped parsley
5 dozen stuffed crawfish heads (see below)
About 7-1/2 cups cooked Louisiana long-grain white rice

Prepare a large crawfish-boiling pot with enough water for boiling the crawfish; add Zatarain's and lemons and bring to a boil. Drop the crawfish in live, and boil for 10 minutes. Ice down the boil and let the crawfish soak in the cold spiced water; the longer you let them soak, the more seasoning will be absorbed.

Break off the tails. Peel the tails, removing the vein but reserving the little flap of crawfish meat that's over the vein. Remove the crawfish fat from the heads (the little yellow glob that's worth its weight in gold) and reserve in a separate container.

Clean 5 dozen crawfish heads for stuffing. The so-called "head" is actually the large red thorax shell. Remove all inside parts, including the eyes and antennae. What should remain is a little tube with two open ends and one open side. Be careful; the shell must be scraped clean on the inside and it can be a bit rough on the fingers. (I'm told that a beer can opener makes this job easier.) Divide the crawfish fat and tails evenly, reserving half for the bisque and half for the stuffing.

Crawfish Bisque

Prepare the stuffed crawfish heads according to the recipe below. This is very labor-intensive, and takes a long time; most folks I know take two days to make crawfish bisque, cooking the crawfish, cleaning the heads and stuffing them the day before, and cooking the bisque on the second day. Recruit some help if you can. Place the stuffed heads in a pan and refrigerate.

To prepare the bisque, make a roux with the butter, oil and flour. Cook over low-medium heat, being careful not to scorch the butter, until the roux turns light brown. Stir CONSTANTLY. This means constantly, without stopping for anything. Add the onions, bell pepper, celery and garlic, and continue to cook, stirring constantly, until the vegetables are soft and the roux is peanut butter-colored. Remove from heat and cool, continuing to stir.

Gradually and <u>carefully</u> add the stock or water (stock preferably) and combine thoroughly, making a nice gravy. Add half of the crawfish tails and crawfish fat, Creole seasoning, salt and peppers, and cook over low heat for 15 minutes. If you've got a little leftover crawfish stuffing, add it to the pot as well, as it adds more body and flavor.

Add the baked or sautéed crawfish heads, and cook over low heat for 30 minutes. Add the onion tops and parsley just before serving.
To serve, mound about 3/4 cup rice in large bowl, and divide the bisque evenly between them. Serve 6 stuffed crawfish heads with each serving.

Don't worry about table manners; you almost have to use your fingers to get the stuffing out of the heads, and I've seen some folks (like me) inserting tongue into crawfish head to lick all the stuffing out. If you want to be more dainty, the tail end of your fork or spoon, or the end of a butter knife, helps get the stuffing out more easily. Make sure everyone gets the same number of heads, or fights <u>will</u> break out; they're that good.

I'm told that tradition requires the empty heads to be placed around the rim of the bowl, so that some don't get more than others. It's easier to count them quickly that way.

Crawfish Monica

1 lb. crawfish tails, boiled and peeled
1 lb. shrimp, peeled
1 stick butter
1 pint half-and-half
1 large onion, chopped
1 cup of green onion
1/2 cup of parsley
4 tablespoons cloves garlic, chopped
1-2 tablespoons Creole Seasoning, to taste
1 lb. cooked fresh pasta

Pre-cook your pasta of choice, drain, and set aside.

In a large saucepan melt your butter and sauté onion and garlic, once the onions are soft add green onion and parsley, continue to sauté' for an additional 2-3 minutes. Continue to stir, be careful that your butter does not burn.

Now add the half-and-half, then Creole seasoning. Cook for 5 - 10 minutes over medium heat until the sauce thickens. Add the pasta and toss well. Let it sit for 10 minutes or so over very low heat.

Crawfish Andouille Pasta

2 pounds crawfish tails, cooked
½ cup diced Andouille sausage
1 pound fettuccini noodles, cooked
¼ pound butter
2 tbsps chopped garlic
½ cup diced onions
¼ cup diced celery
¼ cup diced red bell peppers
¼ cup diced green bell peppers
1 cup sliced mushrooms
½ cup diced tomatoes
¾ cup flour
1 quart crawfish stock (see method below) or 1 quart water seasoned with chicken bouillon
¼ cup dry white wine
1 tbsp lemon juice
¼ cup tomato sauce
1½ cups heavy whipping cream
1 tsp chopped basil
1 tsp chopped tarragon
2 tbsps chopped parsley
¼ cup sliced green onions
salt and black pepper to taste

In a heavy-bottomed 3½-quart saucepan, melt butter over medium-high heat. Add garlic, onions, celery, bell peppers, mushrooms, tomatoes and Andouille. Sauté for 5 minutes or until vegetables are wilted. Sprinkle in flour and blend well.

Whisk in crawfish stock, white wine, lemon juice and tomato sauce. Whisk well until all is blended. Bring to a simmer and hold for 10 minutes, stirring frequently. Add crawfish tails and cream.

Return to simmer and cook 10 minutes. Add basil, tarragon, parsley and green onions. Season to taste with salt and pepper. Remove from heat and toss with pasta.

Mom's Shrimp Creole

Vegetable oil
5lbs. of shrimp
2 large onions, finely chopped
4 cloves of garlic
2 bunches of green onion
2 green bell peppers
1 red bell pepper
1 bunch of parsley
2 cans of whole tomatoes
Salt, cayenne pepper, black pepper, and Creole seasoning to taste

Drain the tomatoes, but save the liquid. Finely chop all of the seasoning.

In a large iron skillet, add 2 tablespoons of vegetable oil, Sauté' your vegetables, after the vegetables are slightly tender add tomato liquid. Stir for about 5-10 minutes, bringing to a boil and add tomatoes.

Bring everything to a simmer, and then add shrimp.

Shrimp Creole Tip: If the consistency is too thick add water. If the consistency is to thin, in a separate glass mix a little cornstarch in some water, once fully mixed add to the pot, and that should thicken it up.

Corte Bouillon

(Coubion)

2 lbs of Catfish Fillets cut into pieces*
4 Tablespoons of Creole Seasoning
4 Tablespoons of vegetable oil
2 Medium Onions
4 Stalks Celery
2 Small Bell Peppers
4 Tablespoon Garlic, minced
2 Cans Diced Tomatoes
Fish Stock, Seafood Stock or water to cover, about 2-3 cups
4 Fresh Bay Leaves
1/2 Cup Dark Roux
3 Lemon Slices
1/4 cup Flat Leaf Parsley, Chopped
1 Cup Thinly sliced Green Onions
Salt, Black Pepper, Cayenne to taste

Toss the Catfish with the Creole Seasoning and keep in the refrigerator.

Heat the vegetable oil over medium heat, add the onions, celery, bell pepper, and sauté. Add the tomatoes and cook for about 1-2 minutes. Cover with the stock by 1/2 inch, add bay leaves, thyme, garlic and a small amount of seasonings, bring to a boil; Add the Dark Roux, cook stirring constantly for 2 minutes.

Lower the heat and simmer about 20 minutes. Stir in parsley, 1/2 of the green onions, Catfish and the lemon slices. Simmer for 30-45 minutes. If the Coubion gets a little too thick add a touch of stock or water, the consistency should be stew like, not watery. Be careful when stirring the pot not to break up the Catfish.

Adjust the seasonings if necessary, remove the bay leaf and lemon slices. Serve over boiled rice and top with the remaining green onions.

Pane' Meat
(Fried Veal)

1 Egg
½ teaspoon Salt
1/4 teaspoon Pepper
2 tablespoons Water
1 pound x Thin veal round, cut into 4 pieces
¾ to 1cup of Italian bread crumbs
Oil to cover bottom of pan

Beat egg, salt, pepper and water together well.

Dip each piece of veal first into egg mixture and then coat well with bread crumbs.

Place in very hot oil and fry on both sides until well browned and meat is cooked through.

Oysters Rockefeller

Although Antoine's restaurant carried the original, this is our version.

1 garlic clove
2 cups loosely packed fresh spinach
1/2 cup chopped green onions
1/2 cup minced onion
3/4 cup (1 1/2 sticks) unsalted butter, room temperature
1/2 cup dry Italian style breadcrumbs
2 tablespoons of anise-flavored liqueur
1 teaspoon Tabasco
1/2 tablespoon Creole Seasoning
1 lbs. of rock salt
24 fresh oysters, shucked, shells reserved
1/4 cup freshly grated Parmesan cheese

Position rack in top third of oven and preheat to 450°F. Finely chop garlic and onion in processor. Add spinach, and green onions to garlic. Process, using on/off turns, until mixture is finely chopped. Transfer mixture to medium bowl.

Combine butter, breadcrumbs, anise-flavored liqueur, and hot sauce in processor. Process until well blended. Return spinach mixture to processor. Process, using on/off turns, just until mixtures are blended. Season with salt and pepper. (Can be made 8 hours ahead. Cover; chill.)

Sprinkle rock salt over large baking sheet to depth of 1/2 inch. Arrange oysters in half shells atop rock salt. Top each oyster with 1 tablespoon spinach mixture. Sprinkle with cheese. Bake until spinach mixture browns on top, about 8 minutes

Grandma's Baked Chicken and Gravy

1 whole frozen (thaw out) or fresh chicken
1/4 cup oil
1/4 cup butter
Salt to taste
Pepper t to taste
1 tablespoon garlic powder

Very simple and tasteful! Organic chicken will probably have the best flavor. Clean and trim fat off chicken. Salt and Pepper the chicken on both sides. Place chicken in large baking pan with skin side down.

Drizzle oil and butter over the chicken. Cover tightly with aluminum foil. Place in oven and bake at 325 for about 45 minutes. Take pan out and carefully turn each piece with fork or tongs......skin side up. Replace foil and bake for another 30 minutes or until almost done. For the last 15 minutes, remove foil and baste the chicken like a turkey, about every 2 or 3 minutes on broil.

Chicken is done when the skin reaches a lovely golden brown. Do not walk away because the chicken will go from brown to black in a heart beat. There should be a nice grease gravy to serve over rice or potatoes. If not add a little water before the basting step.

Enjoy with broccoli or spinach! -Janet Rochon

Mimi's Smothered Chicken in Mushroom Gravy

1/4 cup butter, melted
1 (3 1/2) pound chicken, cut up
2 cups sliced onions
1/2 cup of bell pepper
1/2 cup of green onion
1/2 cup of celery
1/4 cup of garlic
1/2 cup of parsley
1 (14 ounce) can condensed cream of mushroom soup
1 (5 ounce) can evaporated milk
1/2 teaspoon salt
1/8 teaspoon pepper
Creole Seasoning to taste
Hot cooked rice

Pour melted butter into an ungreased 13-in.x 9-in.x 2-in. baking dish.

Place chicken, skin side down, in baking dish. Cover chicken with onions, celery, green onion, garlic, parsley, bell pepper, and the soup mixture. Sprinkle with salt pepper, and Creole Seasoning. Reduce heat to 325 degrees F Cover and bake 20 minute or until juices run clear.

Once cooked, uncover, turn chicken pieces; and let bake an additional 20 minutes, or until golden brown.

Serve over rice if desire.

Alexis's Breaded and Baked Pork Chops

8 pork chops
1 box seasoned Croutons
1 stick Butter
1/2 cup Garlic
1/2 cup Green onions
1/4 cup of parsley
Onion powder
Salt
Pepper

Clean pork chops thoroughly.

Place in baking pan and season both sides, marinate in salt pepper, garlic, and butter.

Place croutons on top of pork chops and pour 1/2 cup of melted butter on top.

Place pork chops in oven and bake at 350 degrees.

Ursula's Crockpot Roast

Sirloin Rump Roast
1 green bell pepper
1 red bell pepper
3 stalks of celery
1 bag of cut carrots
2 bunches of green onion
1/2 cup garlic
1 red onion
1 can of cream of celery soup
1 stick of butter
Creole seasoning to taste

Okay so this is the EASIEST recipe in the book. So easy we are going to do the entire thing in 4 steps!

Step 1: Chop all your seasoning

Step 2: Season your roast with your creole seasoning, then put your roast, chopped seasoning, butter, and cream of celery soup (just dump it on there! Don't reread SERIOUSLY! Just dump it on there) in the crock pot. (Night before is preferred, store it in the refrigerator overnight)

Step 3: The next morning, earlier the better, take your roast out of the refrigerator and turn the crock pot on.

Step 4: Walk away from it.

Set the time depending on the size of the roast. You know it's done when it start falling apart in the crock pot. Thank me later!

Auntie Mimi's Baked Spaghetti

2 bags of elbow macaroni
1 lbs. ground beef
1 can of tomato sauce
1 can tomato paste
1 green bell pepper
1 cup parsley
1//2 cup green onion
1/2 cup of onion
1/4 cup of garlic

In one pot bring your pastas to boil , drain, place back in large pot and let cool.

In a separate cast iron skillet, sauté your chopped parsley, green onion, onion, and garlic with the tomato paste until cooked down. Once fully sautéed add ground beef and continue to stir.

Once ground beef is cooked, add your cooked meat mixture to your pot of macaroni. Add the can of tomato sauce and stir thoroughly. Add 1/2 sharp cheddar cheese and continue to stir. Once it's mixed pour your mixture into a large baking dish.

Cover the top with cheese. Place foil over the casserole and place in oven for 15 minutes and bake at 350 degrees. Once cheese is completely melted , remove foil. Let casserole bake for an additional 5 minutes until golden brown.

Remove and serve.

Cabbage

1 large head of cabbage
1 large onion
1 bell pepper
1 ham hock
6 teaspoons of Creole seasoning
3 bay leaves
Salt and paper to taste

Combine all ingredients in a Dutch oven or heavy saucepan and cook, covered, until cabbage is tender (about 1-1/2 hours).

Peeled and quartered potatoes may be added for the last 20 minutes of cooking time.

When cabbage is done, remove the ham from the bone, cut into bite-sized pieces and serve with the cabbage.

Remove bay leaves before serving. May be served in soup plates or bowls.

Fried Seafood Po~Boys

Pick your desired seafood:
Soft Shell Crab
Shrimp
Oysters
Catfish
Scallops
Calamari
Clam Strips

Create your seasoning:
Onion Powder
Garlic powder
Creole seasoning
Salt
Pepper
Cayenne Pepper
Parsley flakes
Seasoned Seafood Fry

You will need the following to dress your Po-Boy:
French Bread
Mayonnaise
Pickles
Butter
Lettuce
Tomatoes
Tabasco sauce (optional)

Heat the oil in a large sauce pan. Season your desired seafood, onion powder, garlic powder, Creole seasoning, salt, pepper, cayenne, pepper and parsley with salt and cayenne. In a shallow pan, combine 1/2 cup of flour. Or seafood fry. Dredge the seafood in the seasoned seafood fry, coating the shrimp completely.

Fry the seafood in the hot oil until golden brown, stirring constantly, about 4 minutes. Remove from the oil and drain on a paper lined plate. Season with salt and hot sauce, (optional).

On a baking sheet split the French bread loaves in half, butter both sides, and place in the oven on broil for no more then 6 minutes. Spread the mayonnaise on both sides of the bread. Build the sandwich with the fried seafood, pickles, lettuce, and tomatoes. Add Tabasco sauce to taste.

Blackened Catfish

6-8 -catfish fillets, thinly sliced
1 teaspoon cayenne pepper
1 teaspoon black pepper
1 teaspoon salt
1 teaspoon Creole Seasoning
1/8 cup ground parsley
1/8 cup ground garlic
1/8 cup ground green onion
1/2 cup butter, melted
lemon juice

Rinse catfish fillets under running cold water and then thoroughly pat dry with paper towels.

Make your seasoning mixture by combining cayenne pepper, black pepper, salt, and ground seasoning in a small bowl.

Brush melted butter lightly over catfish fillets and rub with blackened seasoning mix. Repeat for other side. Be sure to completely coat each fillet.

Heat iron cast skillet until it is very hot, about 10 minutes. Pour the leftover butter into your skillet. Carefully place the catfish fillets into the skillet and cook for about 4 minutes on both sides.

This blackened seasoning mixture will produce some smoke so another way to tell when to turn over your fillets is when the smoke turns gray.

Big Gio's Turkey Marinade

Recipe for 15-20lb turkey
4 large yellow onions chopped
8 stalks of celery
2 cups of green onion
2 cups chopped parsley
1 cup of garlic
1 can cream of celery soup
2 green bell pepper
2 red bell pepper
4 sticks of butter
Liquid Injection marinade
Creole Seasoning

The night before you cook the turkey. Inject the turkey with your choice of marinade, chop all seasoning and place inside the turkey with the 4 sticks of butter.

Sprinkle lightly with creole seasoning, Pour the cream of celery soup on to of the turkey. Store in refrigerator until you are ready to cook.

Omari's Fried Turkey & Marinade

1 (16 ounce) bottle Italian dressing
1/2 cup green onion purée
1/2 cup onion purée
1/2 cup parsley purée
1/2 cup garlic purée
Creole seasoning
Salt
Cayenne or Black pepper

In a medium bowl, mix Italian dressing, green onion, onion, parsley, garlic, and desired seasonings. Rub over turkey, using remaining Italian dressing to fill cavity. Allow turkey to marinate 8 hours, or overnight, before deep-frying as desired.

Dad's Barbeque Chicken

Chicken Pieces
Creole Seasoning
Salt
Pepper
Cayenne Pepper
Onion Powder
Garlic Powder
Parsley Flakes
Lea & Perrins Worcestershire sauce for Chicken
Barbeque Sauce

In a large bowl Season Chicken thoroughly! Toss the chicken with onion powder, garlic powder, salt, pepper, cayenne pepper, Creole seasoning, and parsley flakes, and Worcestershire sauce.

Barbeque Tip: Best when marinated over-night

Place the chicken on grill over medium heat. Cook the chicken for 15 minutes, remove it from the grill and then brush liberally, coating every inch of the pieces with the barbecue sauce

Return to the grill for 25 to 30 more minutes, basting the chicken for a second time half way through remaining cooking time.

Serve with extra sauce.

Making Groceries
A Story of Creole Cooking from a Creole Family

King Cake

1 box Hot Roll Mix, 16 ounces
1/2 cup granulated sugar for filling
1-1/2 teaspoons cinnamon for filling
1/3 cup unsalted butter, room temperature

Preheat oven to 375°F.

Cream the butter, sugar, and cinnamon together until soft enough to spread easily. Follow directions on the Hot Roll Mix package. Turn one half of the dough onto a floured surface, and roll into a 2-foot x 1-foot rectangle. Spread half of the butter and filling mixture on top of the dough. Beginning at the wide edge, roll the dough toward you into a long cigar shape approximately 2 inches in diameter. Do the same with the second half of the dough. Taking a good thing a step further, many bakeries now stuff their King Cakes with ingredients such as apple, peach, or cherry pie filling, cream cheese, or chopped pecans with cinnamon sugar. Use your creative imagination.

Place dough roll seam side down on a well greased baking sheet, and curve each roll, pinching the ends together to make oval ring. Cover, and let rise in warm place for 20 minutes or until doubled in size.

Bake at 375°F for 15 to 20 minutes or until a straw inserted into the dough comes out clean. Allow the cake to cool.

GLAZE
2 cups confectioners' sugar,
2 tablespoons lemon juice
2 tablespoons water
1 cup granulated sugar, large crystals
3 or 4 drops purple food coloring
3 or 4 drops green food coloring
3 or 4 drops yellow food coloring

To prepare the glaze, combine sugar, lemon juice, and water mixing until smooth. Slowly add more water by the teaspoon until it spreads as easily as a thin icing.
Place 1/3 cup sugar in each of three small jars with lids. Add three drops of food coloring in each one. Cover with lid, and shake until color is evenly distributed throughout the large sugar crystals. Add food coloring, drop by drop until the desired shade is achieved.
Coat the top of the oval king cake with glaze. Immediately sprinkle the colored sugars in 2- to 3-inch alternating rows of purple, green and gold. Cut and serve.

White Chocolate King Cake

1 box Hot Roll Mix, 16 ounces
1/2 cup granulated sugar for filling
1-1/2 teaspoons cinnamon for filling
1 Bag White Chocolate chips
1/3 cup unsalted butter, room temperature

Preheat oven to 375°F.

Cream the butter, sugar, and cinnamon together until soft enough to spread easily. Follow directions on the Hot Roll Mix package. Turn one half of the dough onto a floured surface, and roll into a 2-foot x 1-foot rectangle. Spread half of the butter and filling mixture on top of the dough.

Sprinkle the white chocolate chips on top of the dough. Beginning at the wide edge, roll the dough toward you into a long cigar shape approximately 2 inches in diameter. Do the same with the second half of the dough. Place dough roll seam side down on a well greased baking sheet, and curve each roll, pinching the ends together to make oval ring. Cover, and let rise in warm place for 20 minutes or until doubled in size. Bake at 375°F for 15 to 20 minutes or until a straw inserted into the dough comes out clean. Allow the cake to cool.

GLAZE
2 cups confectioners' sugar,
2 tablespoons water
1 cup granulated sugar, large crystals
3 or 4 drops purple food coloring
3 or 4 drops green food coloring
3 or 4 drops yellow food coloring

To prepare the glaze, combine sugar, lemon juice, and water mixing until smooth. Slowly add more water by the teaspoon until it spreads as easily as a thin icing.

Place 1/3 cup sugar in each of three small jars with lids. Add three drops of food coloring in each one. Cover with lid, and shake until color is evenly distributed throughout the large sugar crystals. Add food coloring, drop by drop until the desired shade is achieved.

Coat the top of the oval king cake with glaze. Immediately sprinkle the colored sugars in 2- to- 3 inch alternating rows of purple, green and gold. Cut and serve

Super Easy Beignets

1 can of biscuits
Vegetable oil
Powdered sugar

Fill a deep cast iron pot with vegetable oil, (you can use a deep fryer as well).

Open your can of biscuits.

Flatten each biscuit out with a rolling pin.

Once the biscuit is flat and round cut it in half.

Place the biscuits in the hot oil and let cook until puffed and golden brown.

Sprinkle with powered sugar and serve.

Mimi's Pralines

> *I loved watching Mimi make pralines….probably more then I liked eating them. I hate pecans. I used to ask her if she could make a few pralines without the pecans… She would tell me. "Girl, I can't make a praline without pecans, if I do then it's not a praline!!" In other words if you don't like nuts, maybe you should make fudge.*

Before you embark on this endeavor, if in fact this is your first time; make sure you aren't doing anything else. You cannot walk away from this pot. This is definitely one of the foods that you have to make with love.

2 sticks of butter
2 cups of cream
2 cups of light brown sugar
2 tablespoons of light corn syrup
4 cups of white sugar
8 cups of pecans

In a large saucepan mix butter, cream and corn syrup; add white and brown sugar and bring to a boil.
Continue to stir, ingredients for 20-30 minutes.

You will know that the praline is ready by this small test. Drop a few drops of the sugary mixture into a cold glass of water, if a small ball firms, then it's ready to be placed on the wax paper. If the ball dissolves in the water or does not stay firm it is NOT ready to be poured….KEEP stirring. <u>Once it is ready pour, add the pralines.</u>

Do not let this sit. It will harden in the pot. Using a ladle; scoop the mixture into individual sized circles onto the paper.

Once they have hardened they are ready to eat.   Enjoy!!!

Wax paper tip:
Wax paper should be placed on top of three layers of newspaper and rubbed down with butter. Newspaper helps absorb the heat, so the pralines cool faster. And the butter keeps then from sticking.

Chocolate Chip Toffee Cookies

1 cup of softened butter
12oz. Of milk chocolate chips
12oz. Bag of Toffee Chips
4 cups of flour
1cups of brown sugar
1 teaspoon of baking soda
1/2 teaspoon of salt
1 cup of sugar
1/2 8 oz. Hersey Bar
2 eggs
1 teaspoon of vanilla
1 teaspoon of baking soda

Cream butter with white sugar and brown sugar.

Add eggs and vanilla, once mixed add flour, salt, baking soda, and baking powder.

Add chocolate chips, Hersey bar and toffee chips.

Mix thoroughly with wooden spoon. If you use a blender you with blend the chips into the cookie dough.

Once mixed, roll the dough into balls, and place two inches apart on a greased cookie sheet

Bake for 10 -15 minutes at 375 degrees.

Makes 2 dozen cookies.

Mimi's Famous New Orleans Rum Cake

This recipe is for everyone that has ever asked Mimi to make you a rum cake, or 2 or 3 at a time... Now you can make your own!

Rum Sauce

2 sticks of butter
2 cups of sugar
1 cup of rum

Heat butter and sugar on low heat, and let it boil for 40 minutes, then turn down, and add rum. Chop 2 cups of pecans

Grease 2 Bundt pans with shortening, STOP.

Grease the pan very well. Or as Mimi, would say..
   "You better get every nook and cranny of that pan otherwise my cake is gonna stick, Let me see, nope you missed a spot right there, da*&t ! give it to me I'll do it myself!"

Sprinkle pecans around the bottom of the pan.

Pre heat oven to 350 degrees

Cake Ingredients

2 boxes of yellow cake mix
2 boxes of instant vanilla pudding
1 cup of oil
1 cup of rum
8 eggs

Mix in Mixmaster for 2minutes at #5 speed…..
For those of you that don't have one, just mix by hand until fully blended….NO lumps. Pour cake mix into Bundt pans and Bake for 40 to 45 minutes

Once the cake is baked, puncture cake in several places and pour half of the rum sauce into the holes. Take the rum sauce and pour it over the cake after you have flipped it over on the plate.

Mimi's Pecan Squares

It's normally the requested that my grandmother make these, wherever she goes. It's either this or the rum cake, most people settle for both.

2 ½ sticks of butter
2lbs of light brown sugar
6 eggs
3 cups of flour
2 teaspoons of baking powder
½ teaspoon of salt
½ teaspoon allspice
½ teaspoon ginger
½ teaspoon nutmeg
½ teaspoon cinnamon
2 cups of raisins
6 cups of pecans

In a large mixing bowl, blend butter, brown sugar, eggs, and flour. After blended add baking powder, salt, and spices. Add the raisins and pecans to the mixture and stir.

Grease pan with butter and flour, so they won't stick.

Bake at 350 degrees for 35 to 40 min.

Cut into squares while warm.

Caution:
Beware when baking these pecan squares. They have been known to attract uninvited company, create long lasting conversation (especially during mail delivery hour), and every now and then have been known to disappear almost instantaneously.

Best served with café' au lait!!!

White Chocolate Bread Pudding with White Chocolate Rum Sauce

6 ounces of melted white chocolate
½ cup white sugar
½ cup of light brown sugar
1 cup of whipping cream
2 eggs lightly beaten
8 egg yolks
1 tablespoon of vanilla extract
1 tablespoon of rum extract
1 loaf of French bread
Raisins (optional)

Melt your butter and out it into a 13x9 pan. Melt your cream white chocolate, vanilla and rum extract; with the heat on medium-low add, sugar, and eggs.

Place the already dried French bread in the 13x9 pan. Then pour the white chocolate mixture over the bread. After the bread has absorbed the majority of the liquid, place foil over it and put it in the oven.

Bake the bread pudding at 275 degrees for about an hour, then remove the foil and let it brown.

Serve with White Chocolate Rum Sauce

French bread tip:
Break the French bread into pieces, and then lay flat on a pan and bake to dry the bread out. Its a lot faster then leaving it out and waiting for it to go stale.

White Chocolate Rum Sauce

10 ounces of chocolate
½ cup of whipping cream
1 tablespoon of vanilla
1 tablespoon of cinnamon
½ cup of rum

In a double boiler melt the white chocolate, vanilla, and cream. After the white chocolate is fully melted turn the fire on low and add the coconut rum. Spoon the chocolate sauce over the bread pudding.

King Cake Bread Pudding with Rum Sauce

½ cup white sugar
½ cup of light brown sugar
1 cup of whipping cream
2 eggs lightly beaten
8 egg yolks
1 tablespoon of vanilla extract
1 tablespoon of rum extract
1 loaf of unfrosted king cake (stale)
Raisins (optional)

Melt your butter and out it into a 13x9 pan. Blend your cream white, vanilla and rum extract; with the heat on medium-low add, sugar, eggs, and raisins.

Try and dust off as much sugar off the king cake as possible. Break the stale king cake up into 1 inch pieces. Place the King Cake pieces in the 13x9 pan. Then pour the cream mixture over the bread. After the bread has absorbed the majority of the liquid, place foil over it and put it in the oven. Bake the bread pudding at 275 degrees for about an hour, then remove the foil and let it brown.

Serve with Rum Sauce

King Cake Tip: If you cannot find unfrosted King cake, you may substitute cinnamon rolls. Bake the cinnamon rolls, and then after they are cooked leave them to dry out in the over.

Rum Sauce

½ cup of whipping cream
1 tablespoon of vanilla
1 tablespoon of cinnamon
½ cup of rum

In a double boiler stir vanilla, and cream, and rum, until blended. Add cinnamon to taste, reduce heat and transfer to serving dish. Spoon the rum sauce over the bread pudding.

Bananas Foster

Bananas Foster
2 tablespoons butter
3 tablespoons light brown sugar
1/8 teaspoon ground cinnamon
1 banana
1 tablespoon almond extract
1/4 cup rum
2 tablespoons king cake vodka

In a small skillet over medium heat, melt butter.

Stir in sugar and cinnamon and heat until bubbly.

Peel and slice the banana. Place banana pieces and almond extract in skillet and cook 3 to 4 minutes more, basting with syrup.

In a long-handled pan, heat rum and king cake vodka over medium heat until just warm.

Ignite the alcohol and pour carefully over the banana slices. Remove the banana pan from the heat and continue to baste the banana slices with their sauce until the flames die down. Serve at once.

Double Frosted Bourbon Brownies

3/4 cup sifted flour
1/4 teaspoon baking soda
1/4 teaspoon salt
1/4 cup sugar
1/4 cup brown sugar
1/3 cup vegetable shortening
2 tablespoons cream
6 ounces pkg. milk chocolate pieces
2 teaspoon vanilla
2 eggs
1 1/2 cup coarsely chopped pecans (optional)
4 tablespoons bourbon

WHITE FROSTING
1/2 cup butter or margarine, softened
1 teaspoon vanilla or rum extract
2 cups powdered sugar

CHOCOLATE GLAZE
6 ounces pkg. milk chocolate pieces
1 tablespoon of butter

Sift flour, baking soda and salt onto waxed paper. Combine sugar, shortening and water in medium saucepan. Heat, stirring constantly until sugar melts and mixture comes to boiling. Remove from heat; stir in chocolate pieces and vanilla until smooth. Beat in eggs, one at a time. Stir in flour mixture and walnuts.

Spread evenly in a 9x9" greased pan. Bake at 325 for 30 minutes or until shiny and firm on top. Remove from oven, sprinkle bourbon over top, cool completely.

Spread White Frosting evenly over top. Chill until firm. Spread Chocolate Glaze over frosting. Chill. Cut into squares. Keep refrigerated until ready to serve.

WHITE FROSTING: Combine all ingredients; beat until smooth and spreadable.

CHOCOLATE GLAZE: Combine all ingredients in top of double boiler. Set over hot (not boiling) water until melted.

Passé Blanc Pecan Brownies

3 tablespoons Instant coffee powder
1 tablespoon half and half
2 cups Brown sugar -- firmly packed
3/4 cup Unsalted butter
2 large Eggs
2 tablespoons Kahlua liqueur
2 cups Flour
2 teaspoons Baking powder
1/2 teaspoon Salt
5 ounces White chocolate -- chopped
3/4 cup Pecans, coarsely chopped

Preheat oven to 350 F degrees. Grease a square baking pan.

Combine coffee powder and water in a heavy saucepan. Stir over medium heat until coffee is dissolved. Add the sugar and butter and stir until butter is melted.

Pour into a large bowl and cool to room temperature. Add eggs and coffee liqueur to butter mixture, stir well to combine. Sift flour, baking powder, and salt in small bowl. Add to butter mixture and stir to blend.

Stir in chocolate and pecans.

Pour batter into prepared baking pan.

Bake until center is set, about 35 minutes.

Cool in pan on rack..

My 7up Pound Cake

4 sticks of butter
3 cups of flour
2 cups of sugar
4 eggs
1 cup of cream
1 teaspoon of salt
1 tablespoon of baking powder
1 tablespoon of lemon extract
1 tablespoon of vanilla extract
1 cup of 7up

Do not melt the butter, but make sure it's soft.

In a large mixing bowl, whip the butter and the sugar until it's fluffy. Then add the cream. Slowly add the eggs in one by one until it's fully mixed. After all of the eggs are added, fold in the flour. Continue to mix until all ingredients are fully blended.

Now add the salt, baking powder, lemon, and vanilla extract, continue to stir. Now add the 7up.

Make sure your Bundt pan is greased well before putting your cake in. I recommend using butter, and then coating your Bundt pan with flour.

Bake at 300 degree's for 1 hour

Pumpkin's 7up Cake

4 sticks of butter
3 cups of flour
3 cups of sugar
5 eggs
1 cup of 7up
1 tablespoon of lemon extract

Do not melt the butter, but make sure it's soft.

In a large mixing bowl, whip the butter and the sugar until it's fluffy. Slowly add the eggs in one by one until it's fully mixed. After all of the eggs are added, fold in the flour. Continue to mix until all ingredients are fully blended.

Now add the 7up and lemon extract.

Make sure your Bundt pan is greased well before putting your cake in. I recommend using butter, and then coating your Bundt pan with flour.

Bake at 325 degree's for 1 hour and 10 minutes.

"Let me know how it comes out," -Pumpkin

Dad & Ursula's Pineapple Upside-down Cake

1 can of pineapple slices
2 sticks of butter
1 teaspoon Cinnamon
½ cup Sugar
1 cup Light brown sugar
1 box of yellow cake mix
1 box of pineapple cake mix
1 tablespoon vanilla extract
1 cup pineapple rum
Cherries

Using a double boiler melt you butter, sugar, brown sugar, cinnamon, and vanilla and let it simmer. Open the pineapple slices and drain them but keep the juice. Add your pineapple slices to the double boiler, let them slightly cook down. Place on low and add the rum.

Using a large black skillet place the pineapple slices around the bottom of the pan. Place cherries in the center of each of the pineapple openings. Using half of the sugar mixture in your double boiler, take a ladle and pour it over the pineapple.

IMPORTANT!!!
Mix your cake mix, HOWEVER!!...Substitute the pineapple juice you saved, in place of the water and, instead of oil use butter.

After the cake batter is completely mixed pour the cake mix over the pineapple and place in the oven to bake.

10-15 minutes before the cake is done take it out of the oven; spoon the rest of the sugar mixture on top. Place the cake back in the oven for the remaining time it needs to bake. The sugar mixture is going to caramelized on top.

"Talk about good!"

Mom's Sweet Potato Pie

2 pie shells
4 cups cooked, peeled sweet potatoes
8 ounces (1/2 cup) unsalted butter
1 cup heavy cream
1 cup light brown sugar, packed
4 large eggs, slightly beaten
2 tablespoon vanilla extract
2 tablespoon ground cinnamon
1 tablespoon ground nutmeg
pinch of salt

Preheat the oven to 400°F (°C). Line a rimmed baking sheet with nonstick aluminum foil.

Pierce the exterior of each sweet potato. Use the tines of a fork to make holes in the skin of each potato, piercing the potato three or four times. Place the pierced sweet potatoes on the prepared baking sheet.

Bake the uncovered sweet potatoes in the oven. The sweet potatoes need to bake until they become tender, which will usually take between 45 - 60 minutes.

After they are cooked mash sweet potatoes with half butter.

Let cool.

Add heavy cream, brown sugar, eggs, vanilla, and all of the spices.

Beat until fluffy; scoop into pie crust.

Bake at 375° for 45 minutes, or golden brown.

Babe's Favorite Pecan Pie

3 eggs
1 cup sugar
1 cup Light OR Dark Corn Syrup
2 tablespoons butter OR margarine, melted
1 teaspoon vanilla extract
1-1/2 cups (6 ounces) pecans
1 (9-inch) unbaked or frozen deep-dish pie crust

Beat eggs slightly in medium bowl. Add sugar, Corn Syrup, butter and vanilla; stir until blended. Stir in pecans. Place pie dough in pie pan. Pour pecan filling into pie crust.

Bake 55 to 60 minutes Cool on wire rack.

To use prepared frozen pie crust: Place cookie sheet in oven and preheat oven as directed. Pour filling into frozen crust and bake on preheated cookie sheet.

Rum Caramel Sauce for Pecan Pie

¾ cup Granulated Sugar
1/8 teaspoon Salt
½ cup White Corn Syrup
¼ cup Butter Or Margarine
1 cup Cream
½ teaspoon Vanilla Extract
½ cup rum

Mix sugar, salt, corn syrup, and butter with cream. Cook over low heat to 250 degrees. Cook on a double boiler, until there is a buttery sheen over the sauce, add the other half cup of cream and continue to stir. Add the vanilla. Add the rum at the end, if you add it too soon you will cook all of the alcohol out.

Looking for a little lagniappe?
Serve with vanilla ice cream, or the ultimate southern favorite pralines and cream ice cream .

Peach Cobbler

4 16 oz. packages frozen peaches
1 cup sugar
1/4 cup brown sugar
1/2 teaspoon freshly grated nutmeg
1 teaspoon cinnamon
1/4 cup flour
3 tablespoons butter

1/2 recipe Basic Pie Crust

Topping (optional):
1 tablespoon milk
2 tablespoons sugar
1/2 teaspoon cinnamon

Place the peaches in a strainer over a bowl; let them thaw, reserving the juice. Transfer the peaches to a 2-3 quart baking dish such as a 9 x 13" shallow glass dish or a 7 x 9" deeper glass dish.

Whisk together the sugar, brown sugar, nutmeg, cinnamon, and flour until smooth. Add 2 cups of the reserved peach juice.
Microwave on high power for 2 minutes; whisk until smooth, and microwave an additional 2 to 3 minutes or until boiling and slightly thickened.

Whisk in the butter and pour over the peaches.

Preheat the oven to 375°.

Roll out the pie dough to a 10" x 10" rectangle; the dough will be quite thick. Using a ruler, cut 1" strips from the dough.
Lay strips horizontally over the peaches, then weave pieces of dough vertically, making a lattice. Trim the edges.
Brush the top with the milk, mix the 2 tablespoons sugar with the 1/2 teaspoon cinnamon, and sprinkle over the top.
Bake the cobbler in the preheated oven for 35-45 minutes or until the filling is bubbly and the topping is golden.

Serve immediately with sweetened whipped cream or ice cream.

Couzan Hazel's Lemon Meringue Ice Box Pie
Thanks to Roxanne...

1 box vanilla wafers
1/2 stick butter
3 eggs
1 can condensed milk
3 lemons
1 yellow food coloring (optional)
Powdered sugar
Cream of tartar

FIRST - Crust
Mash 1/2 box of vanilla wafers fine. Mix crumbs with melted butter and flatten into pie pan (bottom and up sides ...) Add whole cookies to edge of pie pan

SECOND - Lemon Filling
Squeeze lemons and strain into a bowl (if you really like lemon, you can add some additional lemon juice to taste ... not too much b/c can taste more tart after it's chilled). Separate egg yolks from egg whites (cannot have any yolk in the egg whites). Place egg whites on the side. Mix egg yolk, lemon juice and condensed milk together (can add food coloring or leave as is). Fill pie pan

THIRD - Meringue
Beat egg whites till fluffy with 1 teaspoon of cream of tartar. Add powdered sugar to taste (1/2 cup should do). When firm (test by pulling out beaters ... if meringue stands stiff, is firm enough) spread on top of filling.

Put in oven at 350 to lightly toast the meringue then...

Refrigerate until serving .

Making Groceries
A Story of Creole Cooking from a Creole Family

Thank You...

Thank You...

Thank You...

Thank You...

Making Groceries
A Story of Creole Cooking from a Creole Family

Thank You...

Making Groceries
A Story of Creole Cooking from a Creole Family

Thank You...

Thank You...

References

- My family
- Brasseaux, Carl. French, Cajun, Creole, Houma: A Primer on Franco phone Louisiana. Baton-Rouge: Louisiana State University Press, 2005.
- Klingler, Thomas A. If I could turn my tongue like that: The Creole Language of Pointe-Coupée Parish, La. Baton-Rouge: Louisiana State University Press, 2003.
- Marshall, Margaret. The Origin and Development of Louisiana Creole French: French and Creole in Louisiana. Ed. Valdman, Albert. New York: Plenum Press, 1997.
- Valdman, Albert. Valdman, Albert, et al. Dictionary of Louisiana Creole. Bloomington: Indiana University Press, 1998.
- Valdman, Albert, Thomas A. Klingler, Margaret M. Marshall, and Kevin J. Rottet (eds.). 1996. The Dictionary of Louisiana Creole. Bloomington, IN: Indiana University Press.
- Louisiana Experience by Mary Alice Fontenot & Julie Landry
- Encyclopedia of Cajun and Creole Cuisine by John D. Folse
- Louisiana Office of Tourism
- www.nolacuisine.com
- Chef John D. Folse, Experience Great Cajun & Creole Food and Recipes; Taking the Taste of Louisiana Worldwide. www.jfolse.com

Making Groceries
A Story of Creole Cooking from a Creole Family

My Family Recipes...

Making Groceries
A Story of Creole Cooking from a Creole Family

My Family Recipes...

Making Groceries
A Story of Creole Cooking from a Creole Family

My Family Recipes...

Making Groceries
A Story of Creole Cooking from a Creole Family

My Family Recipes...

Making Groceries
A Story of Creole Cooking from a Creole Family

My Family Recipes...

Making Groceries
A Story of Creole Cooking from a Creole Family

My Family Recipes...

Making Groceries
A Story of Creole Cooking from a Creole Family

My Family Recipes...

Making Groceries
A Story of Creole Cooking from a Creole Family

My Family Recipes...

Making Groceries
A Story of Creole Cooking from a Creole Family

My Family Recipes...

Making Groceries
A Story of Creole Cooking from a Creole Family

My Family Recipes...

Making Groceries
A Story of Creole Cooking from a Creole Family

My Family Recipes...

Making Groceries
A Story of Creole Cooking from a Creole Family

My Family Recipes...

Making Groceries
A Story of Creole Cooking from a Creole Family

My Family Recipes...

Making Groceries
A Story of Creole Cooking from a Creole Family

My Family Recipes...

Making Groceries
A Story of Creole Cooking from a Creole Family

My Family Recipes...

Making Groceries
A Story of Creole Cooking from a Creole Family

My Family Recipes...

Making Groceries
A Story of Creole Cooking from a Creole Family

My Family Recipes...

Making Groceries
A Story of Creole Cooking from a Creole Family

My Family Recipes...

Making Groceries
A Story of Creole Cooking from a Creole Family

My Family Recipes...

Making Groceries
A Story of Creole Cooking from a Creole Family

My Family Recipes...

Thank you for reading Making Groceries. I truly hope that it will bring joy and happiness to you and your families life. Don't hesitate to leave a review on my Amazon or Barnes & Noble comment forums. I would love to hear from you! Be on the look out for more books just like this one and more. All titles can be previewed at Printhousebooks.com

PRINTHOUSEBOOKS.com
Read it! Enjoy it! Tell A Friend!
Atlanta, GA.

www.ingramcontent.com/pod-product-compliance
Lightning Source LLC
Chambersburg PA
CBHW080607090426
42735CB00017B/3360